AVOIDING EXTINCTION: REIMAGINING LEGAL SERVICES FOR THE 21ST CENTURY

AVOIDING EXTINCTION: REIMAGINING LEGAL SERVICES FOR THE 21ST CENTURY

MITCHELL KOWALSKI

Avoiding Extinction: Reimagining Legal Services
for the 21st Century

iUniverse books may be ordered through booksellers or by contacting:

iUniverse
1663 Liberty Drive
Bloomington, IN 47403
www.iuniverse.com
1-800-Authors (1-800-288-4677)

ISBN: 978-1-4917-9315-2 (sc)
ISBN: 978-1-4917-9316-9 (e)

Library of Congress Control Number: 2016905462

Print information available on the last page.

iUniverse rev. date: 04/20/2016

For Maia and Max

The illiterate of the 21ˢᵗ century will not be those who can't read and write, but those who cannot learn, unlearn, and relearn.
— Alvin Toffler, *Rethinking the Future* (Rowan Gibson ed., 1997)

Should you find yourself in a chronically leaking boat, energy devoted to changing vessels is likely to be more productive than energy devoted to patching leaks.
— Warren Buffet, quoted in Mary Buffett & David Clark, *The Tao of Warren Buffett* (2006)

The tone at the top determines the tune in the middle.
— Yilmaz Argüden, "Measuring the Effectiveness of Corporate Governance," *Insead Knowledge,* April 15, 2010

If you don't want to be the horses' hoof prints, you got to be the hooves.
— Bruce Cockburn, "Incandescent Blue," on *Dancing in the Dragon's Jaws* (True North Records, 1979)

ACKNOWLEDGEMENTS

My thanks to Joanne Horibe, MaryLee Farrugia, Jordan Furlong, Tim Brandhorst, and the ABA anonymous readers for their comments on early drafts of this book. Thanks to Mike Greidanus for his comments on procurement and to Thomas Pastore at Guardian Industries for sharing Guardian's expense guidelines. Discussions generated by the class and instructors of the Association of Corporate Counsel's Value-Based Billing Program held in Washington, D.C., on July 13 and 14, 2010 were extremely helpful as were those discussions at the Directors Education Program jointly run by the Institute of Corporate Directors and the Rotman School of Management at the University of Toronto, and discussions at the Integrative Thinking Program run at the Rotman School of Management. Thanks also to the writers at Toronto Writers' Centre who gave me constant encouragement, especially Ania Szado. Big thanks to Roz Spafford for her many editorial comments that helped make this a better book. And finally, special thanks to my beloved wife, Yvonne, for all your love and support.

PREFACE TO THE
ORIGINAL EDITION

Avoiding Extinction: Reimagining Legal Services for the 21ˢᵗ Century is based on a cover article I wrote for the July/August 2009 issue of a Canadian legal magazine called *National*. Since that time, the legal profession has made some minor evolutionary changes yet remained maddeningly the same.

We now live an era of innovative legal entities such as Clearspire and Axiom, online documents provided by LegalZoom, publicly traded law firms like Australia's Slater & Gordon, legal process outsourcers like Pangea3. It is also an era where alternative business models in the United Kingdom are creating franchise law offices in retail shops, yet most law firms around the world still practice law the way it has been practiced for centuries; a labor-intensive endeavor carried out by high-priced personnel billing by the hour. Protected by legislated monopolies, law firms have been allowed to grow complacent, fat and inefficient.

While it is hard to pinpoint the first moment at which businesspeople and some lawyers began to question the old, established way in which law has been practiced, certainly one of the first writers to challenge the notion of law firms as unassailable purveyors of legal services is Richard Susskind. His most recent book, *The End of Lawyers?*, has become the source of new thinking about legal services delivery. Susskind's book contains a wealth of fresh ideas about legal services delivery; however, the most profound takeaway in his book is the following:

*Law does not exist to provide a livelihood for lawyers
any more than illness exists to provide a livelihood for
doctors. Successful legal business may be a by-product
of law . . . but it is not the purpose.*

For me, these sentences are at the core of all my thinking
on innovation in law. And it will not surprise readers that these
sentences are also at the heart of Sylvester Bowen's innovations
at BFC. What has been lost on many within the legal profession
is that the ability to deliver legal services is not a right, it's a
privilege—one that lawyers must earn every day. If lawyers do
not earn that privilege, clients will turn to other service providers.

I thought highly enough of *The End of Lawyers?* to include
it as part of the curriculum of an LL.M. course I was teaching
at Osgoode Hall Law School in Toronto in early 2009. My
students—a mix of new and older lawyers—had predictably
mixed emotions about the book. Some were quite guarded about
their right to exclusively practice law while others welcomed
innovation particularly in more commoditized areas of law such
as real estate. Shortly after I finished teaching this course, Richard
Susskind arrived in Toronto as a stop on his book tour. His book
was politely received by many lawyers in Canada, then promptly
put on their bookshelves—unread. The lack of innovation and
thoughtfulness in Canadian law firm operations continued
without missing a step.

Inspired by *The End of Lawyers?* and astounded by Canada's
lack of enthusiasm for Susskind's book, I wrote my piece for
National. It was crafted as a speech given by the managing director
of a fictitious law firm in which she explained the success of her
law firm. The feedback I received on the article, particularly from
young lawyers, indicated that there was an entire generation of
lawyers who were dissatisfied with how their firms were practicing
law. Several readers told me that they were fooled into believing

that my "ideal" law firm really existed and sought to apply to it—until they came to the conclusion of the article. As a result, I decided to flesh out my thoughts about the law firm of the future in book form—to show law firms what they would look like if they recreated themselves to provide better, faster, and cheaper legal services. You now have that product in your hands or on your screen.

Avoiding Extinction: Reimagining Legal Services for the 21st Century is unique not only because of its narrative form, but also because it is the only book that puts all the pieces together. There are a number of books, articles and blogs written on various aspects of legal innovation. However, to my knowledge, no one has put those theories/innovations all together and reassembled a law firm in its entirety. Alvin Toffler's 1980 bestseller, *The Third Wave*, was based in part on the premise that major business breakthroughs come not from single, isolated technologies but from imaginative juxtapositions, developed through large-scale thinking and the application of general theories. In other words, breakthroughs come from those who see the big picture. It is through *Avoiding Extinction: Reimagining Legal Services for the 21st Century* that I have sought to take a big-picture look at the way legal services can be better provided.

I have been asked by many if an existing law firm can change into a BFC law firm. The answer is: yes. Adopting the efficiencies and other ideas discussed in this book are not impossible. The greater challenge however, will come in doing away with the practice of billing by the hour. Compensation and career advancement in most firms are tied to the number of hours billed by a lawyer. When billable hours are done away with, firms will be forced to restructure how they pay their lawyers and how lawyers will advance within the firm. They will be forced to consider the types of behavior that they want from their lawyers and design compensation and advancement models that drive that kind of behavior. I believe that this type of change will be successful only if a firm adopts a corporate structure. And it will most certainly require strong, focused, and committed leadership—but it is possible.

The discussions in *Avoiding Extinction: Reimagining Legal Services for the 21st Century* are not limited to a specific legal jurisdiction so that they may better resonate with businesspeople, general counsel, and lawyers throughout the world. Businesspeople and general counsel should read this book with a view to pushing their firms to be more efficient. Lawyers should read it to determine how they can create a better business model.

Are there areas of this book that do not drill down specifically to explain every nuance of the concepts described? Yes, of course there are. Keep in mind that *Avoiding Extinction: Reimagining Legal Services for the 21st Century* is not meant to be a reference book to be taken down from a library shelf on an as-needed basis. It is designed to be thought-provoking rather than definitive. In those instances, where more information is required it is for the reader to source it out.

Readers of early drafts of this book have had different reactions to its characters. Some lawyers have said that their lives bear no resemblance to that of the characters in the book, while others have said that they thought the book had been written specifically about them. The diversity of experience among lawyers is such that no single character can possibly capture it all, and so the characters in *Avoiding Extinction: Reimagining Legal Services for the 21st Century* can be nothing more than vehicles through which to illustrate my thoughts about an ideal law firm—and also to add an element of fun.

Finally, as I noted at the beginning of this Preface, the reader should bear in mind that many of the innovations discussed in this book are not science fiction. Although no law firm has yet created a real-life version of BFC, many firms are using one or more of the ideas discussed in this book; and many of these innovations are in use by various other industries. The Legal Services Act in the UK, which came into full force just before the publication of *Avoiding Extinction: Reimagining Legal Services for the 21st Century*, will deliver some astounding examples of how legal services can be better provided.

The legal profession is now entering the most inventive and disruptive period of change that it has ever experienced.

Keep watching. The fallout will be exciting.

Christmas, 2011
Toronto, Canada
Mitch Kowalski

PART I

CHAPTER 1
Maria's Dilemma

Maria Fernandez, general counsel for Kowtor Industries, tossed her pen on the desk, sat back in her chair, and sighed. She hated to bring work home and when there was no way around it, she had a standing rule to keep things light. Tonight she had already dealt with a pressing contract matter; now she was settling in to review a large invoice from one of the many outside counsel she used. After that, she wanted to take another look at the RFP response by Bowen, Fong & Chandri, PC.

As Maria swiveled her chair to pull a thick file folder from her briefcase, she heard a loud shout from her kids as they played video games downstairs—another reminder that she was failing as a mother. At least in theory, working in her home office made her closer to her children.

Rising up from her desk, Maria caught her reflection in a plaque hanging from her home-office wall: *The Hispanic National Bar Association's Latina Attorney of the Year, 2011.* "A pioneer," the president of the HNBA had called her that night. "A superb general counsel and a shining example of what a strong and wise Latina woman can do." Tonight, however, she felt neither strong nor wise. And if the reflection was any indication, she looked like hell; every day seemed to add more lines around her eyes, more strands of gray hair. In her reading glasses, she looked older than her mother. *Latinas are supposed to keep our youth as we age,* she thought, then scowled at the image.

She heaved the folder onto her desk, accidentally hitting the "start" button on her blood pressure monitor. The arm band began to inflate. She clicked the stop button, pulled the folder in front of her, and started to read, red pen at the ready to strike out duplicate entries, blatant overbilling, and valueless time. However, her mind wandered back to her company's recent annual meeting.

"We anticipate another year in which the global economy will continue to be on life support," Kowtor's European managing director had put it, "and so it is absolutely critical that all business units do their part to reduce costs wherever possible." Harry Kow, Kowtor's founder, had closed the meeting with a reiteration of those words; it did not go unnoticed that he looked directly at Maria when saying so. It was clear that legal costs would no longer been seen as a necessary evil, shrugged off as the cost of doing business; the legal group would not be exempt from doing its part to improve Kowtor's bottom line.

Retail sales had not rebounded and that was putting pressure on the manufacturing end. All the while, counterfeiters and trademark rip-offs seemed to be on the rise—as did Kowtor's seemingly insatiable need for legal services. Maria was doing her best to keep her team of in-house lawyers to no more than six professionals per billion dollars of revenue. But as Kowtor Industries' annual revenue approached $3 billion, she had an in-house group of twenty lawyers, a group that was threatening to grow larger. The alternative was to send even more work to outside lawyers—but that would play havoc with her budget.

Maria shook her head to clear her mind so she could focus on the statement of account in front of her, for outside legal services related to the acquisition of facilities in Puerto Rico. In short order, she circled two time entries for the same partner, on the same date. Total time: twenty-nine hours. Besides the obvious impossibility of anyone working more than twenty-four hours in a single day, Kowtor's outside counsel policy did not permit any law firm to bill more than twelve hours per day without prior approval; no such approval had been granted on this file. She suppressed the urge to slash the entries with a flood of red ink; instead, she circled them both and wrote in the most girlish scroll she could muster, "How'd you do it?" She followed the notation with a happy face. The sarcasm would be much more biting, she thought, if she were blonde.

She flipped to the end of the account statement—page 80— to see the total fee. Maria blinked her eyes hard to make sure that she was reading the amount properly. She hadn't expected the bill to be small, but this was outrageously high. Plus, it was late. *What's wrong with these people?* Maria thought. *Don't they want to get paid?*

More importantly, Kowtor's finance group was going to go ballistic! They hadn't accrued anywhere near this amount of money in the legal budget for this quarter. The statement was two months later than it should have been, and this was the second time this year for this firm. *Do they think that we make up attorney guidelines because we have nothing else to do? That the guidelines are optional?*

It seemed to be a never-ending struggle, with Kowtor always having to be on its guard from abuse by law firm billing practices. Maria was tired of an adversarial relationship with outside counsel who seemed to be focused solely on how much they could charge Kowtor for that particular year. She didn't want to be a cop; she wanted to be a partner.

She had already instituted a number of tactics to corral her outside counsel and force them to provide better value to Kowtor; but Kowtor's outside counsel guidelines and an aggressive expense policy had resulted in only minor improvements in law firm behavior.[1] Maria had also been able to achieve additional cost savings by using geography to her advantage, sending legal work to lawyers in lower-cost parts of the country rather than to those who charged big-city fees; the savings were good, but more needed to be done.

She tossed her glasses to the desk and rubbed her eyes before taking in the scene around her; the accounts, the contract work, the blood pressure machine. Photographs of her kids—taken at events she wasn't able to attend—seemed to mock her for being an absentee mother.

Ping!

She turned to her computer. It was an e-mail from Michael, her associate general counsel—second in command for the legal department.

Chief,

I just found this on YouTube. Apparently Bowen was speaking at the Mega Ideas Conference last week.

Worth a look before you meet with his crew about the RFP.

Cheers,
Michael

Maria clicked on the YouTube link, and there was Sylvester Bowen, CEO and chairman of Bowen, Fong & Chandri, perched on a stool in front of a plain white backdrop, center stage. After a tight close-up, which showed a small microphone clipped to his ear, the camera pulled back as Bowen began speaking:

---

[1]   An excerpt from the Kowtor expense and disbursment policy is in Appendix A.

There are countless law firms around the world. Many are very successful. However, our recipe for success is far different from theirs.

We are successful because we believe in challenging the status quo.

We are successful because we believe in changing the nature of how legal services are delivered.

We are successful because we relentlessly search for ways to leverage technology and professionals in order to service our clients' legal needs.

We are successful because we don't benchmark against what others are doing—we reimagine the entire process.

Bowen stood up and walked to the front of the stage.

But why, in a world that is flooded with law firms, have we achieved success? Are our lawyers more highly skilled? Are our lawyers the most highly paid? Do we charge the cheapest fees? Do we perform legal functions that no one else can?

The answer to all of these questions is: no.

We are successful because our clients not only buy what we do, they buy why we do it.[22] Our clients see our passion and they want to be part of our drive for innovation. Seems like an odd thing for a law firm client to want, isn't it?

I'll let you in on a little secret. Our goal is not to do business with every single client on the planet. In fact, we don't want to do business with every single client on the planet—even if we could resolve all the conflict issues.

---

[2] *See* SIMON SINEK, START WITH WHY: HOW GREAT LEADERS INSPIRE EVERYONE TO TAKE ACTION (Portfolio, 2009).

We want to do business with those who believe in what we believe.

People are naturally curious. They like to see and hear about new ways of doing things even if those things aren't in their industry. It's the innovation and creativity that excites them. Our clients want to see that we are as innovative as they are. They want to see that we want to make our services better, faster, and cheaper—that the laws of economics also apply to legal service providers. They want to see that we don't abuse our monopoly by providing average service at high prices.

In the traditional law firm model, there is immense pressure on lawyers to pound out more billable hours each year; to work harder in order to make more profits. This mindset inhibits innovation. It encourages each lawyer to act in his or her own self-interest rather than in the interests of the firm as a whole. It encourages the pursuit of short-term profits at the expense of long-term stability and profitability. This mindset encourages lawyers to see the firm as nothing more than the sum of its parts instead of something that is greater than the sum of its parts.

This old-school thinking was successful at first; and that success bred an arrogance that reinforced the notion that we were practicing law in the correct manner. Couple this with the fact that lawyers are trained to be slaves to precedent, to revere the past, and Marshall McLuhan's famous quote comes true: "We look at the present through a rear-view mirror. We march backwards into the future."

In my view, firms that do not change their business model and embrace innovation are dousing themselves in gasoline and marching along a burning platform to their own destruction.

That is why BFC is different.

When we hire lawyers, we hire those who believe in what we believe.

We don't hire lawyers who are technically good and need a job.

We don't hire lawyers who are driven by money. We hire lawyers who are motivated by our principles of change and innovation.

We don't want lawyers who are seduced by the reliability of hours and profits per partner, because that leads to resistance to change.

We want lawyers who challenge everything, every day; who don't see the world or their practice as a zero-sum game.

We want lawyers who are passionate about why we do what we do, because then great things are achieved.

BFC is committed to be a growing, vibrant place in which to work—that's how we attract top talent.

We know that we can only ride each innovative wave for so long before we need to find the next one, so we place innovation above profitability; we continually invest in ourselves. We redeploy our capital to ensure that we always do find that next innovation. We reward those who create value for the firm no matter how value is created.

These concepts laid the foundation of our success.

The camera panned to the side of the stage where a man was sitting beside a small table and a lounge chair. He invited Bowen to sit for a short interview. This, Maria knew from watching videos of previous conferences, was the informal part of Mega Ideas—the portion that sought to humanize the speaker.

The interviewer started.

Q: You spoke a great deal about how BFC operates, but many of our audience would like to know just how BFC came to be. Can it be replicated without starting from scratch?

A: Replicated? We don't have a monopoly on good management ideas, and so any firm with a strong, committed leadership is able to do what we do, but hopefully by that time BFC will have evolved into something even better [laughs]. In all seriousness, there is nothing stopping any firm from turning itself into BFC. Will it require effective change management as the entire business model is turned on its head? Yes, definitely. New bases for remuneration and advancement will have to be created which have nothing to do with the number of hours billed. My father died at the age of sixty-four because he refused to change his lifestyle. He was quite obese and enjoyed drinking and eating whatever he wished. When he started having the inevitable string of heart attacks and mini-strokes, his doctors warned that he had to drastically change his life if he wanted to live past sixty-five. He ignored their advice. Likewise, law firms today are still able to operate as they do and survive. But eventually it will catch up with them as it did with my dad. Total transformation of an old-style firm will be challenging and difficult, but the alternative is death.

As for starting from scratch, that's not an entirely accurate statement. Fong, Chandri, and I were mid-level associates at a seventy-lawyer firm called Garfield & Carmichael—very unhappy mid-level associates, I might add. And to add to our disgruntled state, the firm suddenly dissolved over Christmas one year. The reasons have never been made clear but our sense was that a majority of partners felt they were making money— just not enough, and they sought greener pastures elsewhere. The remaining partners decided that the firm was not viable as a smaller entity. And so the vote was to dissolve. As associates we were shocked, but after a few days I pulled Fong and Chandri aside and proposed that we start our own firm with as many remnants that we could find from G&C—ten of us, as it turned out. But we would do things differently.

The three of us recognized that a shift had occurred in the legal landscape; possession of legal knowledge was no longer sufficient to ensure the success of a law firm. Legal knowledge, in and of itself, was in fact becoming less valuable. And being smart was just not enough. Add to that, increased competition from non-traditional service sources: accounting firms, paralegals, consultants, in-house legal departments, and legal process outsourcers. Traditional law firms were like lobsters sitting in a slow boiling pot; they had no idea that they were on the cusp of extinction.

The key to survival was better processes and greater efficiency—constant innovation in the delivery of legal services, not only so legal work could be conducted at more affordable pricing, but also so lawyers could provide more client care than they would otherwise be unable to. Accounting giant KPMG had a mission statement that was something to the effect that: *We exist to turn our knowledge into value for the benefit of our clients*. I loved it!

So, for us at BFC, our competitive advantage is created when legal knowledge is innovatively and cost-effectively applied to a specific problem.

Q: There must be many lawyers who see you as a heretic, perhaps even a danger to the profession.

A: The greatest danger to the legal profession comes from those who resist change—typically older partners with retirement on the near horizon. Being willfully blind is not just dangerous to your colleagues within the firm, it's the epitome of selfishness.

Q: You've talked a lot about the firm and its ideals. But most firms are driven by a small group of so-called superstar lawyers or rainmakers, which makes the concept of a firm somewhat erroneous. Doesn't it?

A: At BFC there are no so-called superstars—we all drive the organization. At BFC you leave your ego at the door and become part of the team. We want humble lawyers, lawyers who share the spotlight. If that's not your personality, you're not welcome at BFC.

Q: But surely salary is a prime incentive for recruiting and retaining good lawyers.

A: If you want steep pay, long hours, high stress, and limited job satisfaction—go somewhere else. At BFC we recruit, inspire, and retain exceptional people with an employee-first approach to law. We use performance-based compensation models and we set out to win the hearts and minds of our employees every single day.

Q: So then BFC is a work-life balance firm?

A: I don't know what that means. We ask all lawyers at BFC to ensure that they have considered the demands of legal practice on their home life. The ability to practice law is a privilege, not a right, and there is an obligation to serve your clients as needed. If you want to be a lawyer—then be a lawyer. If you want to be a stay-at-home parent—then be that. Law is not a career that one can simply set aside and pick up whenever it is convenient to the lawyer—at least not without significant financial consequence. Your professional life and your personal life are never going to live without conflict. No lawyer has ever had it all, whether male or female.[3]

---

[3]   *See generally* Karen S. Sibert, *Don't Quit This Day Job*, N.Y. TIMES, June 12, 2011, at 9, www.nytimes.com/2011/06/12/opinion/12sibert.html (similar comments with regard to the medical field).

Q: You mentioned that you don't benchmark against other firms. But surely at some level you must have to do that. Even for the sake of marketing to new clients.

A: Differentiating ourselves from our competitors is different from benchmarking against them. We can differentiate ourselves quite easily, but we do not look to them as benchmarks and measure our performance against theirs, because their business model is fundamentally flawed and so any benchmarking is a false reality for us.

The way we differentiate BFC from our competitors is similar to the way a boutique hotel differentiates itself from larger hotels; not on price but by its services and how it conducts itself. A speech given by Isadore Sharp, when Sharp was still CEO of Four Seasons Hotel, resonated deeply with me. Sharp said, "If we give our customers value, our customers will give us profit." Four Seasons found that customers wanted luxury, but luxury was not solely defined by fantastic surroundings and exquisite meals. What clients valued most was the luxury of time; they wanted something that allowed them to have more time to enjoy a vacation or something that made their time more productive.

I realized that general counsel, who make up the majority of BFC's clients, were no different from those hotel customers. What they also wanted was the luxury of time so that they could better manage their personal and professional lives. They wanted results, but they also wanted a law firm that made their lives easier and one made them look good to their business colleagues.

Q: There must be more to that story.

A: Well, my experience at Garfield & Carmichael did shape one other element of BFC—that of legacy. Garfield had been dead for years at that point, but Carmichael was crushed when he saw the firm

*he built suddenly crumble into dust. His life's work evaporated
and he left nothing for the next generation. When Fong, Chandri,
and I stood among the ashes, we vowed to create something that
would have the potential to last longer than a partnership that
was vulnerable to the pettiness and greed that had destroyed G &
C. We sought to create a firm that would be greater than the sum
of its parts; a firm that would not be hurt when a lawyer left;
a firm that would, by virtue of its philosophy and processes, be
able to survive long after we were dead; a firm that would never
depend upon the personality of any lawyer for survival. Hence the
corporate model of law firm management was created with an
independent board of directors to manage the firm.*

Q: So there really is some ego at BFC? [laughs]

*A: Touché! But ego only in the sense of leaving things in better
shape for the next generation. There is a practical element to the
corporate structure that achieves not only our egotistical needs
[laughs] but also creates success. Truly successful law firms will
be those that can combine an ability to respond to a changing
market with scale. Agility means moving to the "cloud" to take
advantage of its scale and technology or it means achieving scale
quickly through home-sourcing or off-shoring. Agility is simply
not possible in a large partnership structure where partners can
derail a proposal because it will reduce their draws.*

*Q: Your ideas are not what one normally expects from the leader of
any law firm. Do you believe that your being a black, gay male
has shaped your thinking? Are you now someone who others can
look to with pride?*

*A: I don't think anyone should look at another man or woman to get
pride in oneself. It's not about having a black or gay CEO, it's
about having a good CEO with the vision and thinking to move
the firm in the correct direction—that is the most important
thing. Good firms need good leaders and it doesn't matter if he's*

maroon or purple. If some see in me a sense of pride that is for themselves alone. Did the fact that I was a clear outsider in the legal world allow me to step away from conventional groupthink on how law firms operate? Yes, I think that helped. Since I was excluded I was free to think freely. I need to be true to myself and not worry about what others think about me. Self-censoring is counterproductive and hurts the firm as a whole.

Q: *Is BFC's goal to be the number one law firm in the country or the world?*

A: *Being number one, whatever that means, is an outcome, not a goal. Our mindset is to keep challenging the status quo and keep pushing ourselves to be more innovative and responsive to our clients. That keeps us hungry, that gives us a desire to get better and prevents us from being fat and complacent. We need to keep asking ourselves, why do we deserve to exist as a law firm?*

Q: *I have heard about your open-door policy and that you are well known for taking all suggestions seriously from everyone in the firm.*

A: *Absolutely, that is critical to creating a good working environment. I check my ego at the door and have a number of open forums with all members of my team. I am the most expendable guy at BFC because I don't operate the business. My role is about leadership, creativity, and vision for BFC. My job is not to practice law—in fact, I haven't practiced in years. My job is to ignite our unique people and culture so that they can continue to deliver breakout innovation in everything we do.*

I abhor yes-men and yes-women. I don't want to know what's going right—I want to know what's wrong and how it can be fixed! I need someone to tell me the flaws in the strategy. And strategy is not about stability in the market, it's about change, about managing the change, and about being ahead of that change. We innovate or we die—it's that simple.

One of the keys to our success is that we are not vested in past legal practices and we are not afraid to move away from them. We measure our profitability by customer and by legal category; with this information we are able to drop customers or exit legal practice areas that do not perform as expected.

At our retreats we challenge ourselves to come up with new ways to provide service—we break into small groups and brainstorm with the wackiest ideas possible, then reconvene and present ideas to the entire firm. Some get shot down, but some have turned into some of our better processes. Creativity is one of the most, if not the most important quality for law firm leaders to have. Successful firms need to be not only nimble, they need to be resourceful, responsive and creative in how they manage their customer relationships.

A knock on the door startled Maria.

"Who did you think it would be?" It was Jeff, her husband. He negotiated his way around several files strewn across the floor and placed a large mug of hot chocolate down on the one bare patch of her desk.

"Oh, I don't know; just watching this video on one of the firms we are interviewing." She looked up at him. "Thanks, honey," she smiled, then managed to raise herself to give him a hug and a peck on his cheek before sitting back down in her chair.

"The kids are ready for bed. They want to know if it's okay to come and say good night."

"Of course," she said, reaching for the mug.

Before she could get up from her desk, Brandy and Rebecca ran in and hugged her. "Good night, Mommy," they chimed together.

"Good luck with your test tomorrow," Brandy said.

"It's not really a test, honey. At least, not for me."

"So, you're the one giving the test?" Rebecca asked. "Like a teacher?"

"Something like that, sweetheart."

"OK, good night, Mom." Brandy left the room, not at all interested in her mother's work.

"What happens if they fail?" Rebecca said, deciding not to follow her sister to bed just yet.

"Then, they don't get to do work with me."

"Oh." There was a pause. Then her face lit up. "Does that mean that we'll see you more, if they fail?"

She hugged Rebecca tight. "Oh honey, we don't want them to fail, because then Mommy will be going even more crazy with work."

"Oh. That would be bad. We don't get to see you so much now." Her voice was low and sad; her words stung Maria.

"Honey, things will get better," Maria answered. "I know that I haven't been able to spend as much time with you guys as I would like. But things will change."

"Promise?"

"Yup," Maria gulped. "I promise."

"Let's let Mommy get back to work," Jeff said as he picked up Rebecca.

After they left, Maria closed her computer browser. She had seen enough of Sylvester Bowen for the night and had an idea of what tomorrow would bring. Nonetheless, she pulled out the Bowen, Fong & Chandri submission, bound much like the other two firms she and her team had short-listed. She flipped though the presentation absent-mindedly, through the biographies, the client lists, and areas of expertise.

Could BFC really be any different?

Or was Bowen just a great salesman?

CHAPTER 2
Six Months Earlier

The e-mail didn't register properly in Maria's mind. Not because there were any grammatical errors, but because the request was so at odds with reality. She read the last line again. "We would like to arrange a meeting at your earliest convenience to discuss an increase in our hourly rates." Increase? Her neck muscles tightened. Instinctively she began to roll her shoulders up and down to relax them.

"Tom!" She called out from her desk.

A thin man with curly hair peered around her door. "Let me guess. You got the e-mail from Rollins and Parker?"

"You know me far too well."

"And in answer to your next question," he continued, "it's only been three months since we sent out the twelve-month rate freeze request to all firms."

Before Maria could respond, Tom held up his hand to stop her. He walked to her desk thumbing through a number of papers in his hands.

"Sixty-five firms responded positively to the freeze—including Rollins and Parker. They would hold their hourly rates for us, because Kowtor is such an excellent client and long-standing business yadda yadda yadda—the usual BS. But it now seems that Mr. Parker needs more alimony for one of his exes, or a new car for his mistress."

He quickly put his hand to his mouth in mock embarrassment. "Oops, did I say that out loud?"

Maria frowned.

Tom returned to a more businesslike demeanor. "And ten stated that 'unfortunately they were unable to comply' and so we 'unfortunately' cut them off from further work. And five we have yet to hear from."

"You scare me," she said.

"It's what I do." Tom smiled. "Now, the request for proposals meeting is starting in two minutes and you really need to get in there to rally the troops. I'll leave the names of the five delinquent firms on your desk for further action."

The Rollins and Parker e-mail had so distracted her that she had nearly forgotten the RFP meeting. It seemed that she was getting more and more distracted with any number of issues that kept arising daily—issues that were keeping her, and her team, from seeing the big picture and from getting a handle on their overall situation. "Fighting gators," was how she described it to her kids whenever she felt out-of-control, racing from one crisis to the next. Today, however, she and her team were going to find a better way to do things. Today, she was going to drain the swamp.

She had set aside the entire morning for an initial meeting on her procurement initiative for legal services, a new idea for the team. Currently, legal services were, obtained in a rather ad hoc fashion. When the need arose, there were seventy firms on the Kowtor list of approved lawyers from which the team could choose, depending upon their needs. But even then, new relationships would inevitably form and new firms got added.

Moreover, at the most recent board meeting, there was continued, not-so-subtle pressure to examine how things were being done in the legal department. "We need to see all departments making improvements to our bottom line," was how it was phrased. The legal department of Kowtor no longer had the luxury of an unlimited budget that could be shrugged off as a necessary evil. So it was time to think about how things were being done and why, time for the team to step back and question the delivery of legal services and map out a better model.

But it was to be more than just a cost-saving exercise. It was also an opportunity for the team to seriously question what services they were receiving, how the services were being delivered, and what the team really wanted and needed from outside lawyers. If they were going to be serious about draining the swamp, they needed to take the position that nothing was sacrosanct. Everything was up for debate and revision.

Maria grabbed a note pad and started toward the conference room. While she wanted to know what all twenty lawyers in the legal department thought, it made more sense to limit this initial discussion to Michael and her three team leaders.

Stephen, she anticipated, would not be shy about giving his opinion on anything—it was one of the reasons Maria liked him. She had been methodical in her approach to building the legal team. Skill set was an important factor but, in her view, there were a lot of lawyers with the technical skills needed to fill her positions. She was more interested in chemistry and personality, wanting people with whom she could have a spirited yet professional give and take, so that the right issues could be fleshed out. Too much agreement was a signal that something was wrong with the team. She didn't want a group of "yes" men or women.

Julia, only a few years out of private practice and from Dewey Stewart, one of Kowtor's many outside legal counsel, would likely only be comfortable with minor changes. She still had several friends at the Dewey firm that she liked to call up with assignments.

Stephanie had a habit of making even the most innocuous issue into a gender battle, which caused significant friction with Stephen, who could rightly feel outnumbered in the department and seemed to enjoy taking as many jabs as possible at Stephanie, just to see her reaction.

As Maria neared the conference room she mentally went through how she wanted the discussion to progress. She expected the meeting to start with complaints or rants so that the group could get the key irritants out in the open before she focused on three key areas: value, behavior, and costs. All of these were interrelated and should feed off each other: firms concerned about value would modify their behavior, which in turn would affect costs. She hoped that her team would be able to build upon these concepts.

Steps from the conference room she could hear that Stephen was already in full form. She pulled up short of the boardroom to listen in on what he had to say.

"What I hate," Stephen's voice echoed down the hall, "is the ridiculousness of being billed for passing instructions." He paused and took a sip of coffee from a large mug. The rest of the group waited, knowing that he was far from finished. The coffee quaff was merely a signal that there was more—much more—to follow. The mug had not fully rested on the table when he began again. "I give instructions to A. A tells B. B then instructs C. But C doesn't really understand and goes back to A for clarification before passing the file off to the law clerk who is really the right person for the task in the first place." Heads nodded around the table. They all had had similar experiences. "Then we get billed every step of the way!"

"Absolutely," Stephanie's voice made Maria smile. The two Stephens, as she called them, rarely saw eye-to-eye on things. She shuddered to think of what was going to happen when the issue of diversity came up. "We need to guard against the nickel and diming. We've given the instructions—we shouldn't have to pay for the broken telephone that goes on within the firm."

"Remember," Julia added, "the clown who sent me a magazine article on the mining operations in New Guinea with a 'Thought you might be interested' note."

"That was nice of him," Stephen replied.

"Sure, until he buried his time for finding, clipping, and sending that article in another account!"

"Was this the same guy," Stephanie asked, "who added your Christmas gift as a disbursement to an account, then claimed he had reduced the time spent on the file by an equal amount?"

"Same guy."

"Cross that firm off the list," Maria said, sensing that it was the right time to enter the room.

"Hi boss," Stephanie said, not missing a beat. "Yup, long gone."

"We're the client, aren't we?" Stephen wasn't finished. "Correct me if I'm wrong, but shouldn't they want to make us happy? Shouldn't they understand that we are the ones driving the bus?"

"But have we been drivers?" Maria responded. "Or merely chauffeurs?"

"Precisely," Stephen said. "Our annual legal budget is enough to make us important. What are we up to now, $50 million a year?

"Yes, give or take a million," Maria said. "For this procurement I thought that we could deal with all our commercial and corporate work, including intellectual property matters, which is about $30 million per year. That way we would have one point of contact for all that kind of work, which makes things more manageable for us. It would also reduce our seventy-firm list to about ten firms. If it goes well, we can address the type of work being done by these remaining firms for litigation and employment matters in a second procurement process. Sound good?"

Heads all nodded.

Stephen started up again. "Okay, then going back to my point, shouldn't we be driving behaviors that we want?"

"You're dead on, Stephen," Maria said. "The purpose of today's meeting is to talk about what we want from our legal services providers. And you will notice that I am not saying law firms. Because it may be that some of our work doesn't have to be done by a law firm. There are a number of legal process outsourcers who are quite good for repetitive high volume legal work. I think that it's unhealthy for us to only consider law firms. We're all lawyers ourselves; can't we manage a nonlawyer legal services provider for routine work? Thinking in terms of law firms, not legal service providers, may actually limit us in our search for the best provider and I don't want to close that door—at least not yet."

"We're looking for a legal services provider as opposed to a law firm," Michael added, "because there are too many law firms that do not provide the service element, at least not the type of service that we want. And if we think of legal service providers in the same way that we think of Kowtor's other service providers, then maybe we can create a better model."

Maria nodded. "In some ways, we have ourselves to blame for enabling and even incentivizing bad practice on the part of law firms. And I don't mean questionable conduct—although we have seen a little bit of that. But we have allowed, and perhaps even encouraged, bad legal service by not focusing ourselves—and in turn, not focusing our firms—on how we want, and need, things to get done. In short, what I want us to do is reimagine what the perfect legal services provider would be like. Forget about law firms and how they currently provide legal services. We need to start from a blank slate and think about how we would like to see law firms provide us with legal services."

"But we can't just ignore how firms provide legal services." Julia said.

"Why not?" Maria said.

Julia frowned. "Because that's the way they do things. Their business model is set up to work in a particular fashion."

"And that's precisely the problem!" Maria replied, slamming her hand on the table. "That's not a good-enough answer anymore. We should be considering the 5 Whys[4] in connection with law firms and look at a way to make our lives, as in-house counsel, better."

The group went unusually quiet at Maria's comment. She had never slammed the table before in a meeting. She had even surprised herself with her zeal. Clearly the stress of working with a legal profession that she felt was broken was taking its toll. She had always been open with her senior team and so she decided to personalize her commitment to change.

"Look," she began again. "I will be brutally honest with all of you and this will come as no surprise to some. I'm looking for a legal services provider to make my life easier. Not only professionally, as in not having to hand-hold, but also business-wise, as in, I don't want to get any more headaches from the board, and most important of all, personally. Marriage, family, and relationships are hard enough without work impacting on them."

"Amen to that!" Stephen said.

They all laughed. "Think of it as a plan to help you out, Stephen," Julia said.

---

4   The 5 Whys method was developed by Sakichi Toyoda as a problem-solving technique at the Toyota Motor Corporation and involves asking the question "why?" at least five times to drill down into what is the root cause of a problem. For example: My legal fees are expensive. Why? Because the law firm used seven lawyers on the file. Why? Because the law firm is inefficient. Why? Because there is no incentive to be efficient. Why? Because the firm makes more money by being inefficient. Why? Because the firm charges by the hour. The 5 Whys force a deeper exploration of issues and can be an effective way to examine a host of organizational and operational matters in order to correct inefficiencies.

"Third time could be the charm," Stephanie added.

"No more marriages," he responded. "Two ex-wives are more than any man should have to bear."

"Yes, as important as Stephen's love life is to our group," Maria said, "let's get back to legal services providers. As an overarching principle, we should be the ones driving the bus in terms of the type of service we want, demand and receive—not the legal services provider."

Stephanie added, "It's like the difference between being the captain of the ship and being a chauffeur. Both drive the vehicle, but who is ultimately controlling the direction in which we're headed?"

"Hmm, not sure about your mixed metaphors, Steph; maybe it's more like the difference between getting on a bus or being taxied to the destination," Michael responded. "If we take the bus, we'll get to the destination but not at the time of our choosing and not using the most direct route. But if we hire a taxi, we tell him what route to take and we can even discuss how we will pay. On the meter, or by some other means."

"Nice," Maria replied. "But one thing is certain: if we don't push for change, change will not occur. Unless we give legal services providers a reason to change, nothing will happen. There is nothing unreasonable about demanding a new model of legal services to fit our needs. But there is going to be a lot of prep work on our part to get this thing to work. We can't just punch out some poorly thought-out RFP. But my sense is that the work we put in during the RFP process will really pay off later."

"Agreed," said Julia. "And the best place to start is fees. Dewey Stewart gives us a 10 percent across the board discount and we should push for others to do the same."

"Sure." Maria replied. "But I'm talking about going beyond—and I don't mean to be offensive, Julia—simplistic billing arrangements.

I want a value-add that is not a discount." Maria walked over to the whiteboard. "I don't see a discount as value. It's a tactic, not a strategy. It's easy. I want to push them to help us. And if they help us and make us happy, they will continue to do work for us."

"I'm past the point," Stephen said, "and I think that we all are, of thinking that any of the lawyers in town have some secret special knowledge. Time to throw back the curtain. The mystique of the Wizard of Oz is so passé."

The lawyers around the table looked at each other, not really understanding what Stephen was talking about.

"Look," he continued. "We all went to law school and practiced in different firms. We know enough about law to not be in awe of the great mystique of lawyers. So, why do we fall for this crap? Is anyone really worth $1,000 an hour? I hardly think so."

"That's not entirely true, Stephen." Stephanie said. "When I call up Fraser Barney for competition law advice, his rate is $1,000 an hour. And quite frankly, I don't mind paying that much because the guy knows his stuff and can give me an answer efficiently and quickly." She looked around the group as she spoke. "Last month I called him in the middle of the afternoon, explained the problem, and asked if there was an exemption to the filing requirement. Right off the top he told me there were three exemptions, but we could only qualify for one. And for that one, he needed to speak to the regulator about it. He said he would call right away. The next morning he called me back—explained that the exemption wouldn't work but that he and the regulator had come up with something else that would achieve the same result. He sent me a bill for $5,000. I was happy to pay it. He spent five value-added hours on it. Someone at half the rate, with less experience, might have spent $15,000 worth of time screwing around with it before coming to the same conclusion, or finally deciding that there was nothing that could be done."

"That's a great example," Maria said. "Now, if he had said that he would charge you $5,000 right off the bat for that answer, would you have still been happy?"

"Of course! It was an important issue to us and one that I didn't expect would come cheap. And in my head, I had ballparked around $7,500 for the fee."

"Then maybe a lawyer's hourly rate is not the determining factor in terms of the value he gives?" It was Michael responding.

"What mattered was that he did the work well, in a timely fashion, for a price that you felt was fair, given the importance of the matter. In other words, from our perspective, there is a decoupling of cost from price. We don't care what it costs the firm to give the advice; we're concerned about the value of the advice. The value we receive determines the price that we're willing to pay. And I think that's Stephen's point."

Maria watched as her team nodded in agreement. "Okay, can we agree that the value of legal services provided to us is to be defined by us? Not defined by the number of hours spent to do the work?"

"Yes," murmured from the group.

She got up and walked to the whiteboard. "We expect a high degree of expertise from our firms, agreed?"

Heads again nodded across the room.

"And to get a good answer, right?"

More nods.

"But how they come up with that answer is their problem."

"Well, I wouldn't say it's a problem," Julia responded.

"Okay, call it their challenge. Or call it whatever you like; just don't ask us to pay for it."

"And," Stephen jumped in, "if it becomes a problem, then that's a firm we don't want working on our files."

Maria picked up a red marker. Across the top of the whiteboard she wrote in large red letters:

VALUE FOR MONEY

Maria looked back at her team. "Agreed? If you don't know the answer, that's fine—figure it out. But we aren't going to pay for the learning curve, nor are we going to pay to train your lawyers. Training lawyers is the firm's job and all training is to be on the firm's ticket—not ours." She walked back to her chair. "What we value is the result, not the time it took to get to that result."

"Wow," Julia said. "That's pretty aggressive."

"Maybe," said Stephanie, "but it'll definitely drive a new model of behavior. Firms will be forced to invest more heavily in knowledge management to save time answering client questions. To use your example, Julia, another client will surely have a similar question and if the law firm is smart it will have catalogued that answer so that it will be at the fingertips of its lawyers for the next client. It could charge $5,000 to the second client but not expend $5,000 worth of resources."

"Sure, but it's not our role to tell the firms how to run their practices. And—" Julia started.

"Wait a minute. Why isn't it our role?" Stephen asked.

"Pardon?"

"Why isn't it our role to tell the firms how to run their practices?"

"Stephen, are we really having this conversation?" Julia's voice was rising. "It's none of our business."

"Maybe Stephen's got something there," Maria said.

"Maria, you can't be serious?"

Maria nodded her head. "When Kowtor finds a new supplier for our products, we certainly do investigate how that supplier runs its business. Our team goes for an inspection, reviews processes, interviews management and we do quality control spot checks. So, why wouldn't we do the same for our law firms?"

Julia did not respond. The others looked at each other trying to consider why law firms should be treated differently from any other supplier. After all, a law firm was simply another supplier of services to Kowtor, wasn't it? That is what Maria had asked her team to consider at the beginning of the meeting: to reimagine what a legal services provider should look like and how it should act. So, why should it receive special status? Why shouldn't it be told how to do work in the way that Kowtor expected? Why should Kowtor accept, without a whimper, the way that legal services are currently provided?

Maria let the silence sit for a moment before speaking. "Let me propose something that covers what the consensus seems to be. We are looking to drive certain behaviors from our provider or providers, whatever we choose to do. Agreed?"

Heads nodded.

"So, shouldn't we determine what that behavior is, and then use those drivers in preparing the RFP?"

The others looked at her for a few minutes. They started to nod their heads in agreement.

"I agree," said Stephanie. "What we were doing before was merely treating the symptoms, instead of the disease. The problem is not high fees or even how those fees are calculated. We've all agreed that we are willing to pay good money for good service, so we must change the behavior of the selected provider so that we are not seen as a money tree. We are a client that cares about and rewards efficiency and effectiveness. So our goal is to drive effective and efficient service."

"How do we do that?" Julia asked.

Maria held up her hand. "We'll get there shortly," she said to Julia. Turning to the group, she asked, "What things are important to us as a company? What are the values that we think our service providers should also adhere to?"

"Environmentally sensitive. Green." Stephen was the first to shout out.

"Sure," Maria said getting up to write it down on the whiteboard. "Should we be supporting law firms that are not environmentally sensitive? If we do, then are we being true to our own values?"

"But it goes farther than that," Stephen added. "If we don't draw a line in the sand and stipulate that we will not tolerate certain kinds of behavior, then who will?"

"It's not unlike boycotts against companies who did business in South Africa during apartheid," Mark added.

"Or boycotts against companies who employ child labor," Maria said.

"Right, if we stop using them, then they'll get the message to change," Stephen continued. "And hopefully our stand in connection with these issues will start a trend that other companies will follow. We can in fact be agents of change through our legal spending."

"Sure, we can change the world," Julia murmured.

"Sarcasm duly noted, Julia," he replied. "Perhaps, or perhaps not, but we can set a benchmark of reasonable environmental compliance and give that a score. Firms that exceed the benchmark will get additional points in the RFP tabulation and that may just be enough for that firm to beat out another."

Julia wasn't entirely convinced. "Well I wouldn't want an environmentally conscious firm to win out over a better skilled firm."

"Absolutely not," Maria stepped in. "I'm not saying that we prefer values to skills. They are all pieces in the puzzle and we can deal with that through a weighting of scores. Maybe environmental or greenness is weighted as only 5 percent of the overall score."

"Other things?" Maria wanted to keep the meeting moving along and knew that things could quickly get off track. "Stephanie? Diversity perhaps?"

"Ha ha ha—how did you guess?" Stephanie replied. "It seems that you do listen to me—though obviously we don't have that issue in this department."

"As a woman, you would think that," Stephen replied.

Maria frowned at Stephen, before adding, "I think we should add a scorecard based on gender diversity. How many women in the firm, how many are partners, and set up a benchmark on that as well."

"And the ethnic makeup of the firm, as well?" Julia said. "Create a benchmark for that as well. It will of course, be pathetically low. Although I think Dewey Stewart is quite progressive in that regard. And yes, Stephen, Mr. Green, we can agree on an appropriate weighting."

Stephen bowed his head to her in mock thanks.

"Agreed," Stephanie added. "Obviously even I'm not looking for a fully diversified firm that does not have the skill level we need. That takes diversity to the point of absurdity. And even Stephen will agree that I am not that absurd."

"Well, not yet," Stephen replied.

"Wait. Let me write this all down," Maria said. "Environment and diversity. Those are the obvious hot buttons. But how about something more in line with our primary driver, value for money?"

"Efficiency," said Stephen.

"Right. That's where we started this conversation. Okay—so how do we deal with that?"

"It goes back to what you were saying about how we treat new suppliers to the company," Stephanie replied. "So, appropriate use of technology."

"Right. What technology is being used to make things more efficient. But there is more to it than software, right? It has to be attitude," Maria added. "A firm can have all the software it likes, but if it isn't used, or used properly to leverage its true potential, then it's useless."

"Ha! I'd love to see a senior partner show up at our beauty contest and try to explain the firm's software!" Stephanie was enjoying this. "When I worked at Hooguels, there were partners who didn't even know how to use e-mail!"

"When I think of technology," Stephen said. "I typically think in terms of knowledge management. So let's review the firm's KM budget is and its KM strategy."

"Whoa, Stephen!" Julia said. "The firms will freak out! They will never discuss their budgets and strategy. I think we're going way over the line now. We're never going to get firms interested in the RFP if we make too many new requests."

"Then maybe they should start acting like other suppliers," Michael added. "As we mentioned before, when Kowtor finds a manufacturer in, say, Shanghai, we go through their factory and kick the tires right? We look at the technology they are using and we gauge whether or not they are always looking to upgrade their technology. It all comes back to the same questions: Why should we treat our law firms differently? What makes them exempt from the same process that every other supplier has to go through? And I'm sorry, but the adage "that's the way it has always been done" doesn't cut it in my book. I want a firm that gets it, in terms of client expectations."

Michael got up from the table and walked over to the whiteboard next to Maria.

"What we want is a firm that is motivated to do things better and strives for greater efficiency every time they open a file." He continued. "Why shouldn't they be required to show us in exact detail why they are the best rather than just showing us a bunch of old transactions that they worked on? If we're just going to listen to them rattle on about old deals, then how much due diligence are we really doing for our company?"

He looked around the room. No one said a word. So he continued. "Don't we have a duty to our shareholders and the board of directors to ensure that we've done our homework? Law firms have gotten a free ride for too long when it comes to really showing clients how they operate. It is all cloaked in professional honor and calling. We're supposed to just trust that they know best how to do our work. That's so patronizing. Quite frankly, they don't have a bloody clue how to do our work in the best way possible."

"Forget it!" Stephen jumped up from his chair. "Time to take charge. If they can't get KM right, or they don't put emphasis on KM, then that drives inefficiency, and they are not the kind of firm that we want. Again it goes to weighting in the RFP. We can benchmark against what we have seen out there." He looked around to see the group staring at him. He slowly took his seat again.

"So, KM," Maria said, adding it to the whiteboard. "And if there are providers that use KM effectively, then we may be able to get access to their KM as a bonus. What about training— professional development? How much emphasis is placed on PD? That affects the firm's ability to do our work in the long run, right? Budget, staff requirements—are there set hours and set programs?"

Julia laughed. "Have you all really forgotten how little effort firms put into these things? You haven't been gone that long from private practice. There is no such thing as a strategy on these matters! It's all so random."

"Fair enough, then that benchmark will be pretty low," Maria said. "And a firm that spends a lot of effort in these areas will pick up bonus points over the others."

"I'd like to see a relatively high weighting on this," Michael said. "Obviously much higher than greenness or diversity. PD really affects a firm's ability to do our work and therefore has a huge impact on us." He paused. "And I like Maria's bonus idea about KM. The firm should provide us with free access to its KM, subject of course to confidentiality. And getting back to PD, the firm should be providing free training sessions to our team. Both of these create definite value for us."

"Not just for our team, but for management as well," Julia added. "Like what we did for a few clients at Dewey Stewart from time to time."

"So, why aren't they doing that for us now?" Stephen asked.

"I'll look into it," Julia said. Eager to change the topic, she added, "But what about the firm's skill set? We seem to be off track on this. Skills should be first and foremost."

"I'm not suggesting that we will end up with a firm that has poor skills but fantastic PD, KM, and ecodiversity policies," Maria said. "My assumption is that we would first prequalify, by skill set, five firms who wish to respond to the RFP. And I would be hard-pressed to think that these prequalified firms would vary so widely in skill set. They are all going to get top marks or close to it. We are looking for skill, but we assume that the skill will be there."

"Okay, but while an average skill set may be acceptable for the firm in general," Stephanie added, "I would be worried about the training factor. I don't want to be dealing with some junior who doesn't know what she's doing because she's being trained on my file."

Julia nodded her head and suggested that the team stipulate that no lawyer with less than five years' experience was to work on a Kowtor file. "Somewhat arbitrary," she said, "but it makes the point that Kowtor's legal work is not to be used as a training file."

"I agree," Stephen said, "but I don't want us to forget about KM and PD. If a firm doesn't get KM and PD right, then it's not a firm we want to use. I see it as no different from a supplier that doesn't invest in new technology and practices. It speaks to efficiency and the ability to give value to us."

"Yes, Stephen," Maria replied. "I wrote that down. Not to worry."

"I guess what we have to realize," Maria summed up, "is that these bonus scores will be tipping points. And what I mean by tipping points is that all things being equal, we will end up selecting the provider that got bonus points on our drivers. Or, a firm that might not be quite as strong in some areas could pick up some points in the other areas. Provided that we didn't score these other factors so that lack of experience would be compensated for in other categories. I'm the one that has to answer to the Board if things go sideways and neither they, nor the shareholders, will care that our law firms are diverse, if the job isn't done."

"I would also like to see something in the procurement package about processes. Is the firm ISO certified or is it using project management techniques? Do we care about that?" Michael surveyed their blank faces.

He explained. "A look at their processes will give us a glimpse, along with KM, into how the firm operates, and their processes affect efficiency. Is the firm making use of legal process outsourcers and technology to better manage work flow and reduce costs?"

Julia interjected again. "Why should we care about that? Seems a bit intrusive. We're really getting into their shorts now."

"We care," Michael said, "because not only does it address efficiency, it reveals the firm's philosophy, its willingness to adjust to a changing marketplace and how it deals with peaks and valleys in work flow. If the firm can't handle things, then we may be in a situation where our work is not done on time, or the firm

35

disintegrates because it did not manage itself properly, which again, affects our work. It is not at all unusual for firms to go bankrupt or close down. The days of assuming that all law firms are well managed and will always be around is long gone. We need to make sure that the firm we pick is solid, and if we can't get financials, then we have to review all aspects of the firm to satisfy ourselves that they have a viable business model. We need to treat law firms like every other service provider."

Maria added, "Would we really give a contract to manufacture part of our machines to an outfit that didn't invest in new technology, or to one where we couldn't be sure they would be around because their business model was risky? We have to remember that the firm we choose not only reflects on the management of this company, both the shareholders and the Board, but also reflects on our department. Do we want the rest of the company snickering behind our backs about the law firm that we chose? Do we want to receive a litany of complaints about the firm? Do we want to read in the paper one morning that the firm has gone under? We need to be extremely picky when this thing goes out. This is what we are trained to do, so let's do it."

"Any other drivers of behavior?" Stephanie asked, eager to move the meeting along.

"I don't know where this would fit," Stephen said, "but the firm should become more in tune with our business so that it fully understands our issues and is able to add value to us. Something that's not chargeable."

"I agree," Maria said. "It's a benefit to us and also to them. The better they know us, the better service they give, and the less chance that we will walk away from that firm and choose someone else down the road."

Michael added, "Maria mentioned this earlier and I'm not sure that it got written down, but I would like to receive access to the provider's KM. Make it an extension of our rather meager KM supply. We don't have the budget to build a comprehensive KM solution or to do a good job of professional development for our team and for the business units. For me that is fantastic value-add."

"Got it," Maria replied. She turned to Julia. "Didn't we have some intellectual property boutique firm give us a free subscription to its research memos?"

"Yes, Jones Hardy," Julia said "I used it a few times to check up on issues. It's a good idea that really adds value. I would like to see more firms do that kind of thing. I don't need to speak to a lawyer to get my answer for every matter."

"I agree, I can read the research or documents myself," Michael said.

"But we haven't addressed billing," Julia added.

"Is it billing or cost?" Maria replied. "Because I'm not sure they are the same. Perhaps we call it cost for now."

"Since most firms still use hourly billing rates," Michael added, "we'll have to use that as a benchmark using typical hourly billing rates. We can sample across about five firms and that will be the benchmark."

"Sure," Julia said. "And then the firms will get points for discounting. Should we look for 10 percent across the board or should we go for a deeper slice?" She was determined to move for discounts.

"I disagree," Stephen replied. "My sense is that a firm gets no points for discounting fees."

Julia stared at him in disbelief. "How else are we going to know we're getting a deal?"

"Discounting is a mugs game," he replied. "It doesn't address efficiency, which is one of our stated values, right? And quite frankly, with discounts, the firm will become even more inefficient when doing the work so that the fee after discounting is what the fee would have been without a discount."

"Are you suggesting that firms are dishonest in their billing?" Stephanie said. "Horrors!"

"Absolute honesty in a billable-hours scenario is not possible," Maria said. "We all know that. And if outside lawyers were honest with you, they would agree. We all came from firms where we witnessed billing practices that bore no relationship to the time spent on a file. Combine that with the inherent conflict of interest between lawyers trying to meet billable-hours targets and clients wishing to have efficient service; you have a recipe for dishonesty. It's not in a lawyer's best interest to spend less time on a file when she has billable targets. Billable hours create an incentive to spend more time on a file, not less. It penalizes efficient lawyers."

Michael picked up on the point. "Discounted hours also affect the lawyers on the file, and the rest of the firm has no compassion for lawyers working on those files. We all remember that we hated working on discounted files; it affected our bonus at the end of the year. Let's not pretend that there isn't a big incentive for a lawyer to pad hours on discounted files. And if there are lawyers out there who deny that this practice goes on in their own firms, then they are either blind or completely out of touch. Besides, we are unlikely to get the best lawyers for a particular file if their fees are going to be discounted. So I agree with Stephen: discounts to hourly billing are not worth any bonus points."

"Also," said Stephen, "we should be looking for a billing or cost system that provides an incentive for efficiency. What that is, I don't really know. My preference is for some sort of arrangement that allows me to budget effectively and accurately for the year and that forces a firm to do things in a manner that is efficient."

"Okay," Julia replied. "But I'm really concerned that the firm won't properly allocate its resources in order to save money and that will end up biting us in the end. We'll get cheap service but it won't be service that we want because it won't be much in the way of service at all."

"So perhaps, fixed-fee billing is the answer," Stephanie added.

"As long as it isn't based on a formula of hourly rates plus some kind of random cushion to protect the firm," Michael said. "Then we haven't solved the problem of saving money and the firm still isn't forced to work smarter, or more efficiently. We'll have the same system and same costs; we've just called it a different name. If a firm comes up with that kind of system then it stays at the benchmark and gets no bonus marks."

"But how else are they supposed to price themselves?" Julia was clearly concerned.

"It's only been in the last sixty years or so," Maria said, "that lawyers have charged by the hour for work. Before that time, lawyers followed law society regulations, which are fairly uniform no matter what country or state you practice in; the fee is to be reasonable given the work involved and may also take into consideration the result obtained. The reality is, as we said earlier, that no matter what hourly rate a lawyer charges, time spent does not equal value received. In addition, lawyers charge different rates for different clients and for different types of work, so there is no clear method of assessing a lawyer's worth since it's constantly changing. Each year, a lawyer's rate goes up by some arbitrary amount. Why? Because the lawyer has become much smarter and more efficient at her job?"

Stephen laughed out loud.

Maria continued. "Is the rate tied to an excellent review that clearly showed that the lawyer is now giving much more valuable advice? Perhaps, but more likely, rates increase in lockstep based on the number of years a lawyer has practiced, simply because she, and the firm, both want to make more money.

"We've all worked in firms and we know that no matter what our rate was, some of the work we did on a file did not in any way correlate to value to the client—that's the reason you get unhappy clients. Clients must see the value in the work being done and so the client's perception of the value of the work needs to be considered. All of this is a long-winded way of saying that flat fees are not simply about estimating the hours to be worked, then fudging that upwards to catch any perceived losses. Our costs—in this case our legal fees—need to be cheaper than the sum of the hours that a law firm would traditionally spend. The object is to force them to reevaluate every step of their processes.

"They cannot stand on the rather arrogant 'This is not the way we do things.' Or 'That is not our policy.' Because, for most firms, no one really understands why they do what they do—it's simply always been done that way and that process has been handed down for generations without question. So, what I'm saying is that it's time for them to start questioning it, or they will waste a lot of time and money blindly following procedures that don't make sense in every situation. Firms should be training their lawyers to carefully think about the things that need to be done for certain files and what can be left out in others. They have to start making choices. Skinny the file.[5] Learn to do only what is necessary. That is the world that we, as clients live in, and it's time that law firms joined our world."

Michael interjected. "And when you think about it, the real value in a lawyer is her ability to work with a client, in making appropriate choices. A good lawyer will say, 'We don't need to bring that motion or discover that person, or bring an action against that company and here's why.' The corollary, of course, is

---

[5]   Patrick Lamb of Valorem Law Group (http://www.valoremlaw.com/) in Chicago has used the term "skinny the file" in nearly every conversation the author has had with him about value-based billing of legal matters.

our conduct as client. We have to agree not to take unreasonable steps just because we have the firm on the hook for a specific fee. It's a two-way street."

"And," Maria added, "the firm that sorts out a way to create the proper checks and balances is the one that will ultimately win our retainer and be a very profitable outfit."

"What we're really looking for," Michael said, "is a cost system that gives an incentive for providers to be more efficient in how they approach projects but also perform at their best. Whatever is used, it must provide an incentive for the firm to be both efficient and provide excellent service. What we want is a firm that partners with us and is willing to invest time and money with us and share some risks. This is how the best relationships are created."

"True," Stephen said. "Managing our relationship and showing leadership in thinking about client service are the keys to building and keeping a relationship with us. It's not just about law."

"We haven't talked about how firms will be evaluated during the term of the procurement," Julia said.

"Actually, we haven't talked about a term, at all," Stephanie pointed out.

"Okay, so what do we think is a reasonable term of the procurement, given the size of our spend?"

"My sense," Michael said "is that it will take a year for the firm and us to mesh and get to know each other. The first year is a throwaway. So, a minimum of three years, because we also want the firms to be interested in a long-term deal with consistent cash flow for them. We need to keep their attention."

The team ultimately agreed on a three-year term with two renewals of two years each, to be exercised at Kowtor's discretion. That way, they reasoned, the winning provider would continue to work hard to get the next renewal.

The team then turned to whether to evaluate the firm on an annual or quarterly basis. Michael wanted to ensure that once the firm had won the contract, there would be penalties and incentives throughout the term to ensure both that good people were staffing the files and that the firm didn't lose interest in the work.

"We need to incentivize them," he said. "We can set KPIs and SLAs—key performance indicators and service-level agreements—on call-backs, meeting deadlines, general satisfaction ratings, reporting, billing, and anything else we can think of. KPIs will be based on what our team and our business units want from a firm."

"As long as we don't so overwhelm them with KPIs and SLAs that they become focused on checking boxes and lose sight of the bigger picture." It was Maria who made the comment.

"That's not my intention. The real purpose of KPIs and SLAs, beyond providing some mechanism for evaluation, is to reward, or punish, a firm. There should be a fee-at-risk component such that if the firm doesn't achieve certain measurables, it gets less money. Conversely, if it achieves the measurables, then it receives a bonus. I want to keep this simple because I'm a simple guy, but also because this concept will blow firms away."

Stephanie liked the idea. "And we can use their scores as a way to evaluate continuous improvement by the firm in key areas on a year over year basis. This will really allow us to properly assess its performance."

They all turned to see Julia's reaction to Michael's carrot-and-stick approach.

"Don't look at me," she said. "If that's the way you guys feel, I'm just one vote. But I think you'll have a real hard time with that concept. The firms will say that if they do the work, they should be paid."

"Then they have to do the work in the way that we want it done," Michael responded. "And the difference is that we are agreeing to be locked into a long-term relationship and give that firm a constant supply of work, whereas before we would simply not use that firm again if we were dissatisfied with the service. We're trying to encourage a long-term relationship that is mutually beneficial."

"Keep in mind, there is also an upside," Maria said. "If the firm does well, it gets an extra, say, 10 percent in fees. Not a bad gig. Firms wouldn't get that in a normal billing situation. So, we're trying to be fair in encouraging good things, while penalizing behavior that we don't want to see. And this all harks back to the original concept of a lawyer being paid a reasonable fee, given the work involved and the results achieved, as well as our primary driver of value for money. We would be working out KPIs and service level metrics with the winning proponent before we sign so that we are all on the same page in terms of what we are expecting and what they are able to provide. If we can't work out the appropriate KPIs and metrics, then we go to the second-place proponent."

"Look at it as a form of risk assumption, Julia," Stephen said. "The party that's most in control of the process should be the one to assume the most risk of things going over budget. The firm is in control of most things in the matter given to it. Sure, it cannot control everything, but it can control its costs and its personnel, which are a huge part of the equation. So, in my view, it is more than fair for the law firm to absorb risk just as it is entitled to receive a bonus by working more efficiently."

"The KPIs should also be aligned with our goals as a company and to our departmental goals, to ensure that we are in sync," Michael said. "They are not going to be generic useless items. For instance, if internally we have some sort of training goal or some sort of communication goal, and the firm helps us achieve that, it will get a bonus. Or, if the firm gives us some value-added advice or process, then that will count for the bonus structure. Ten percent of $30 million is a nice chunk of change—a pretty good carrot."

"Let me also introduce a final wild card category to this," Maria said.

"Sure, why not," Julia said. She was clearly not going to be surprised by anything at this point.

"We've danced around the subject in a lot of our discussions but let's simply say it out loud. I would like to see a separate scoring category for a specific value-added proposal. Make them tell us straight-out what they can do for us for no additional charge."

"I like it," said Stephanie, "as long as it's something that we can actually use. Like, say, access to their knowledge management database as Michael mentioned or access to professional development program for ourselves and our businesspeople."

"Or something completely out of the box that really helps us out," said Stephen.

***

The sun had almost sunk below the horizon as Michael walked with Maria to the parking lot. "Now that we've created this beast, is there actually a provider that can meet, or, as the marketing types like to say, exceed our expectations?"

"You're reading my mind," Maria said. "Just going over the firms we currently use, I don't see it. Maybe we're shooting way too high, being far too innovative in our approach." She opened her car door and heaved in her briefcase. It was going to be another long night at the home office.

"Well, if we don't find such a firm or provider, at least it will solve one problem," Michael called to her from his car.

"What's that?"

"What to do with all our free time."

CHAPTER 3
BFC Presentation Day

The cab deposited them midway between a hot dog vendor and a rumpled mass fast asleep on an exhaust grate. Those streaming into Urbex Tower's glass and marble facade—well dressed and clutching morning coffees—didn't seem to notice either of them.

"Who buys hot dogs at 9:00 a.m.?" Harry Kow, founder and CEO of Kowtor Industries, scowled as he eased his girth onto the sidewalk. He'd been relatively quiet on the ride in, checking his BlackBerry and reading the newspaper. Maria knew it was too good to last. He was typically most outspoken in the morning, as if he spent the night dreaming up new tirades to unleash upon the world.

By design, each presentation for Kowtor's legal work was made at the office of the relevant short-listed law firm. Maria wanted to see each firm's premises, staffing, and technology. Also, spending time in each office gave her a sense of the firm's culture and personality. The drawback was Harry. He insisted upon coming to each presentation. Like many founders of companies, he found it difficult to let go of any major decision, although he assured Maria that he would "leave the final selection up to the legal department."

Reflecting the morning sun, the neighboring office towers looked like beacons of gold. The message was not lost on Harry. "Could they have found office space in a more expensive area of the city?" he mused loudly. "I can't wait to see our first account." He looked around the street to get his bearings. Another sneer.

"Remind me not to come here for meetings. Parking is going to be out of the stratosphere." He shielded his eyes and moved closer to the building's shadow. "I hate these guys already."

Maria rolled her eyes and smiled at the cab driver as she paid the fare. If Harry was looking for a reaction from her, he wouldn't get it. Better to let him blow off steam now, before the presentation. She had often thought that Harry complained about everything in order to show his concern for value. But he also clearly enjoyed being a grumpy old man. Grey hair and advanced years, he once told a friend within her hearing, gave him freedom, license, "and even an obligation" to say and do things that anyone younger would be severely chastised for. Today it seemed, would be no different. Maria followed Harry into the tower, trying to ignore his muttering.

Finally, just inside the lobby she pulled at his arm. "Harry, this is the last one. We short-listed three for one reason and one reason only. I knew that you couldn't sit through more presentations. I wanted five—"

"Five? Maria, are you completely insane? Why not just inject me with Ebola? Or tie me naked to an ant hill covered in honey? Presentations from five law firms? Good God!" His face turned red with a mixture of mock horror and anger. She had seen that face many times, but after eight years as general counsel she was no longer daunted by it. She was no longer the mousy woman he could intimidate by raising an eyebrow. And although he would never admit it, Maria thought that he liked the fact that she simply ignored his rants and gave back as good as she got. They made a good team, his impulsive, emotional personality melding with her quiet, reasoned approach.

"When I started Kowtor Industries, we used Mike Stewart and his small office near the Bentmart subway station. No muss, no fuss, and no outrageous fees. There was a small bakery with fresh banana bread muffins and cappuccinos next door. Street parking galore. . .."

"Harry," she guided him to the elevators, "enough. That was in 1980 and Mike has been retired for twenty years. Times change and $30 million is a pretty significant procurement. I want to make sure we do our homework." Maria stabbed the call button and turned back to him. "Don't forget. I'm the one that has to live with these people day in and out—much more so than you."

"Yes, I've got that," he said entering the elevator. "But really, Maria—they all say the same thing: 'We're the best!' and 'Here are all the huge files we've worked on and if we're good enough for the others, we're good enough for you.' Honestly, you could change the firm name on the presentation and it would apply to any of the so-called seven sisters. It's like trying to choose between fifty flavors of vanilla. The last two—"

"This firm isn't one of the seven sisters," she interjected. "They claim to be"—she paused to find a better word but couldn't—"different."

"Great. We're here to see the poor cousin."

Harry stopped talking when the elevator opened on the tenth floor to let in a woman pushing a service cart of food. She got off at the twelfth floor.

"And another thing," Harry started, once the doors had closed. "I'm tired of sitting through a presentation where they bring out their $1,000-an-hour stars—as if anyone is worth that kind of money—and then later dump some green kid on us. But whenever the big shot needs a few more hours, he slathers it onto our file as consultation."

She pursed her lips and silently willed the elevator to move faster.

The elevator arrived at the thirtieth floor and opened to a sleek reception area, tasteful and well done, but bereft of any hint of overexpense. Two receptionists sat side-by-side, each with a welcoming smile. Behind them hung three large stainless-steel letters: BFC.

"If I ran our business like that," Harry continued, lowering his voice, "we'd be closed in a month."

"Harry," Maria gritted her teeth as they approached the desk, "we're here, be nice."

"Damn thieves, that's what they all are," he whispered.

"Shhh!"

They identified themselves to the nearer receptionist, who directed them to take a seat in the waiting area next to large windows overlooking the lake. Mr. Bowen, she said, was expecting them and would be out shortly. Maria declined her offer of coffee, tea, or water, then ushered Harry toward the sitting area.

She pulled BFC's written submission from her briefcase, flipping to the score sheet. A fair, consistent, and methodical assessment of each of the three applicants was vital to the procurement process. In this regard the team spent a great deal of time creating a scorecard and a scoring methodology.

All of the senior legal team members had taken part in scoring the written submissions and in making up the short list of three firms. References of the short-listed firms were conducted by Stephen and Stephanie. Presentations from these firms would be made only to Maria and Harry. This would ensure consistency of scoring and minimize disruption to the legal department. "We can't close our department for every presentation," Michael had told the rest of the team, himself disappointed at not being able to see the presentations.

BFC's presentation would be scored, like the others, based on a standard format and agenda, with specific sets of questions to be asked of each proponent. For each question Maria's team had already come up with a list of possible answers, all of which had been prescored, allowing for consistent scoring and comparables.

Presentation scoring included a scoring of the actual persons from the law firm making the presentation; the presentation was to be made only by those lawyers or staff who would actually work Kowtor's file. This would allow Maria and Harry to meet and interview the individuals with whom they would be directly working—preventing any "bait and switch." Michael was very concerned, as was Harry, that a firm would make the presentation with its top lawyers, or with those lawyers who were best at presentations, but that Kowtor would later find that the actual work was done by some unknown lawyer or staff. As a result, if there were personnel at the presentation who would not be working on Kowtor matters, deductions would be made to the scoring.

Like the other firms, BFC had followed the Kowtor procurement format, listing its specialties, client list, and the firm's points of contact. As expected, BFC's marks for technical skill were in line with others Kowtor had reviewed. BFC had the usual list of large corporations who used the firm for everything from major corporate acquisitions to shareholder disputes, employment issues, tax matters, and significant litigation. What was quite different, at least on paper, was the very un-law-firm-like approach to how work was processed, delivered, and priced. BFC's approach had intrigued Maria and the rest of her team, but she had deliberately withheld that information from Harry in the hope that it would make him more attentive at the BFC presentation.

She looked up from the submission to see Harry craning to look down a hall that ran the length of the floor. "Must be the 'deal floor,'" he whispered using his fingers as quotation marks as he said the words. "Nothing but boardrooms and small conference rooms."

"Sit down and stop spying around. You're like a little kid." Maria began to worry about how disruptive he would be during the presentation. Maybe she should have gone to all the presentations with Michael instead. Harry had the attention span of a gnat at the best of times, and the other two presentations had clearly taken their toll on his willingness to properly assess this last firm. His earlier comment about fifty flavors of vanilla was not far off the mark given the last two presentations. There was very little to distinguish those firms from each other. Maria was mentally crossing her fingers that BFC would live up to its apparent uniqueness. "We'll get a tour later," she said to Harry.

He ignored her. "Miss," he called out to the receptionists. "How many floors do you have here?" One of the women replied that this was the only floor at this location.

"The only floor?" he said to Maria, obviously taken aback. "At this location?" He peered around the floor and then faced Maria again. "Where the hell do they keep everyone? Didn't you say they had over 200 lawyers?"

"I told you they were different." She motioned for him to sit but he waved her off.

"Miss, how many locations do you have?

"In the city? We have two locations, sir. This one and the main office at Davenport."

The look of confusion on Harry's face was one Maria had never seen before. He had clearly not read BFC's submission very carefully and was geared up for confrontation with a firm that he thought was a carbon copy of every other he had seen. But now, he seemed lost. Perhaps her plan to keep him in the dark until the presentation was a smart move after all.

"Here's an idea, Harry. Why don't you let them give their presentation and, if you have any questions, you can ask them at that time." She patted the chair next to her. "Deal?"

He was still muttering "the only floor?" as he sat down beside her.

Maria noticed a glossy legal magazine on the table beside her. The magazine was one that had gained a great deal of notoriety—and profit—as being nothing more than a thinly veiled vanity rag for major law firms. On its cover was a photo of Sylvester Bowen that had been cropped into the shape of Herman Miller's Aeron chair. She flipped to the article, skimming it for any information that she didn't already know from the presentation materials. Midway through the piece one of Sylvester Bowen's quotes caught her attention:

> *When the Herman Miller Company set out to create the world's best chair, they cast aside all previous assumptions and started from scratch. The result was a chair that didn't look like a chair.[61] But that chair—the Aeron—has now become the iconic representation of a modern chair. That is BFC in a nutshell. We cast aside all previous notions of what a law firm should look like, how it should act, and how it should be managed. We started from scratch and thought about what clients were looking for in terms of service and what would be the best organization to achieve that goal. As a result, we are the law firm that doesn't look like a law firm. We are the law firm that doesn't act like a law firm. And we are the law firm that certainly does not operate like a law firm. By being the antithesis of the traditional law firm, our goal is to become the iconic representation of the Twenty-First Century Law Firm: the Aeron of law firms.*

Maria was too engrossed in her materials to notice Sylvester Bowen approaching from one of the hallways.

---

[6] Roger Martin uses the Aeron chair as a classic example of innovative or design thinking in his book *The Design of Business*.

"Ms. Fernandez? Mr. Kow?" he called out as he moved forward with an outstretched hand. "I'm Sylvester Bowen. Welcome to BFC and thank you for the opportunity to bid on your RFP."

Maria stood up. "We're pleased to be here to listen to your presentation, Sylvester." She paused for a moment as she studied his features. There was something familiar about him. "Didn't we meet at an Association of Corporate Counsel event last year?"

He looked at her a little more closely. "Possibly. I was on a panel discussion regarding alternative billing last September in Chicago."

"Yes, that's it. We didn't meet but now I do remember you from the panel."

"Great," said Harry, unhappy at not being the center of attention. "Now that the two of you have reconnected, perhaps we can get on with this?"

Bowen was not at all taken aback by Harry's gruffness. "Certainly, Mr. Kow. Please follow me."

As they followed Bowen down the hallway, Harry couldn't keep from muttering to Maria, "A few years ago this guy would have been serving us coffee. Now he's running a law firm."

"Harry!" Maria grabbed him by the arm and stopped him dead. She whispered sharply. "Quiet! He's going to hear you! And can we please stop the racist comments? At least until we get back to the cab? They roll off my back very easily, but these people don't know you."

"It's not racism if you hate everyone equally," he replied.

"We're just set up at the end of the hall," Bowen called out to them. He had continued walking ahead, seemingly unaware that the two had stopped. "If you look to your left you can see our hoteling area."

The two guests hurried forward to where he stood waiting for them. They looked blankly at two rows of long desks fitted with lamps, cabling, and electrical outlets.

"It's unfortunate that we don't have anyone using the space at the moment so you could get an idea of what goes on here. But essentially, as you may already know from the background materials that we submitted, we have a very liberal approach to workspace at BFC." He bit back a smile when he saw Harry Kow's eyes widen at the mention of the word "liberal." "Liberal," Bowen continued, "in the sense that we see the entire planet as workspace for our people. Not to take away any thunder from the presentation that our team is about to make to you, but the hoteling space is space where lawyers can work without being in our office proper in the suburbs. Everything they need to work is here; electricity, comfortable and professional desk space, printer, Internet. It's a veritable plug and work area."

He looked directly at Harry. "In other words, our staff and lawyers can choose to work here at the hub instead of going to the spoke office. They just plug and—"

"Yes, I got it." Harry scowled. "Plug and work, Plug and play. I'm old, not stupid."

"Absolutely, I didn't mean to insinuate that you were stupid, sir." Bowen replied with just enough politeness to ensure that the apology was accepted but far from making it obsequious.

"Just old," Maria couldn't resist. "Really old."

"Sure—gang up on the old white man. Just remember who signs the checks."

Bowen smothered his laugh. He could see through Harry's façade and the fact that Maria was able to poke fun at the old man made him feel more relaxed, but still respectful of Harry. Kowtor would be an excellent addition to the BFC family of clients and he was mindful of the fact that even with all the cost-savings and efficiencies in the world, if Harry Kow didn't like the firm for any reason, the work would go elsewhere. In any event, Maria would be the point person on the file and her reputation of being tough but fair on outside counsel was reassuring.

"Right," Harry said moving the conversation along. "So you have the hoteling space here, and what seems like a bunch of boardrooms. Standard fare, I think."

"Correct. Nothing new about having boardroom space. The innovation, and that is a word that you will hear a lot in the presentation, is in the location of our spoke, which is outside of the central business district to take advantage of lower costs."

"I like your thinking, Bowen," Harry said. "A law firm that actually pays attention to costs. And I assume you pass the savings on to us, right?"

"Yes, in an indirect way. Again, not to steal any thunder, but our view is that the more that we are able to control our costs, and the more that we are able to predict our costs on files, then we are better able to perform legal services in a cost-effective way for our clients. The more uncertainty there is in our costs and in how we manage our files, the higher the cost burden to the client."

Harry nodded his approval. "Maria, these guys actually get it."

"But it's more than just costs," Bowne continued. "Moving out of the core allows us to use space—in our case, old warehouse space—that is more appealing to our staff and closer to where they live, and that in turn reduces our carbon footprint. Again, Maria, please don't take this as our presentation. I realize that one of the stipulations in the RFP is that the presentation is to be made by the lawyers who will actually be the key contacts on your file. I don't practice any longer since taking up the CEO role here at the firm. But I wanted to be the first point of contact today and be able to lead you into the presentation."

"Not to worry, Sylvester. I'm not marking our discussions and even if I wanted to stop Harry from asking questions and wait for the formal presentation, it would be impossible to do so."

"Yes," Harry said. "Always remember whose name forms part of the corporate logo."

Bowen led them into the boardroom at the end of the hall. The room was unremarkable, with a large table in the center and screen at the end of the room. A projector hung from the ceiling.

"I'll leave you two now," Bowen said. "It's important for you to get to know the team that will be responsible for your files without me sticking my nose into things. They are the ones that have to earn your trust and confidence, not an old guy like me. Now—" He looked around the room. "Well it doesn't look like any of our staff are here. Can I get either of you anything to drink before the team comes in?"

Maria shook her head. "No, I'm fine for now, thanks."

He then looked directly into the eyes of Harry Kow. "Coffee, perhaps?"

PART II

CHAPTER 4
BFC's New Hire

The first thing that struck Mark about the subway poster was not the word *syphilis* that jumped from the headline scripted in a tawdry font, but the squid-like creature that was squeezing a young man in its grasp. *On the Rise and Looking for You*, the small print screamed. Making the scene even more surreal was the man in business-casual attire, sitting directly beneath the poster, calmly reading the morning's newspaper, completely unaware of the horrible STD monster just above his head. A small headline in his newspaper—about Japan's snow monkeys—caught Mark's eye. He followed it down the page to a photograph of the creatures sitting comfortably in a hot spring, steam rising around bushy, snow-covered heads. The absurdity of it caused him to smile.

The man suddenly looked up.

"Everything okay?" he asked.

Mark wasn't sure how long he had been staring at the article but it seemed to be long enough to unnerve the man.

"Yes, of course. Sorry for staring. I was fascinated by the snow monkey piece. I had never heard of them before now."

The man turned the paper back toward himself to see what it was that Mark was talking about. "Oh, right. Interesting group." The man's voice had a slight accent.

English, Mark thought. Or perhaps, Australian. He was never good with accents, except the most pronounced and obvious ones.

"I had a chance to see them for real a few years ago," the man continued, "on my way back from the Philippines. I have a few pictures of them in my office. Kind of old hat for me now."

He paused and looked Mark up and down for a moment. "You look familiar. Have we met?"

Mark took a harder look at the man, noting the moustache and short, tousled hair. He did look familiar, but Mark couldn't place where he had seen him. "You may be right about that. We must have come across each other somewhere. Or it's just some random recognition from the subway."

The pair reviewed possible chances of meeting; associations they were part of, sports activities, schools, none of which held anything in common for them.

"Must be completely random then" Mark said. "Off to work?"

"Yes," said the man. "Next stop—I'm at BFC."

"Ah! That's it then," Mark replied. "I'm starting at BFC today. We must have seen each other when they were touring me around last month."

"Oh right! You're the new guy, Mark . . ."

"Reynolds. Mark Reynolds."

"Well, Reynolds, Mark Reynolds, I'm Stephen Boulder. You're sitting just down the way from me actually; mine's the desk with all the snow monkey photos." He paused for a moment. "There's really not that many, just, hmm, five." He looked Mark up and down, again, taking note of Mark's three-piece suit and handkerchief. "A bit overdressed, don't you think?"

A pang of fear ran through Mark.

"I mean, it's a good look," Boulder said. "Don't get me wrong. But we're more casual, unless there are client meetings."

Mark didn't reply. He was calculating how much time it would take him to return home and change. He looked at his watch. He was due at BFC in twenty minutes; he would never make it. He cursed loudly in his mind.

"Not to worry, Mark." Boulder looked out the subway window to get a sense of where they were on the line. "You have about thirty seconds to tell me about your life before we arrive. Married? Kids? House in the suburbs? Cottage?"

"Not quite all of the above. My wife and I have two: a boy, eight, and a girl, five. And Lincoln Park is not really the suburbs. But it's more affordable than a small shoebox downtown and it has a bunch of parks and stuff for the kids. Close to the subway and, as it turns out, BFC."

"Yes, the sat office has its advantages."

"Sat office?"

"Sorry, satellite office. It's what we call it even though that's pretty much where everything happens. The main office downtown is just for show: for clients and closings. The big clients like to have expensive art and mahogany tables for bigger deals— they just don't want to pay for it!" He laughed, then continued. "Although most clients prefer the sat office as it's more reflective of our philosophy. Simple, understated elegance, like Audrey Hepburn in a little black dress."

Mark nodded with a smile, picturing the actress in *Breakfast at Tiffany's*. "I like that. Nice metaphor. It's that kind of understated elegance that attracted me to BFC."

"Really?" Boulder frowned. "Are you giving me the standard HR answer, Mark?"

The subway pulled to a stop.

"Right, here we are." He got up and led Mark out of the car. "You've already got the job, mate. No need to BS me."

"You're right, and I'm not. Actually, what I really like is that BFC is practicing law in a new way."

"Okay, I'll bite. But let me be Socratic about it. What exactly was the old way?"

They walked out of the station onto a street filled with an assortment of small shops, restaurants, cafés, and a small grocery store, the kind that one would find in any small town. In the distance rose the towers of downtown.

"Well, Professor," Mark began, "the old way was logging hundreds of billable hours a month in order to stave off a call from the managing partner, all in the vain hope of making partner. And once you made partner, you would continue to beg, borrow, or steal hundreds of hours per month at a much higher billing rate in order to keep an absurdly high draw." He drew a breath, amazed at the mouthful of words he had just expelled. Ahead of them was a squat industrial building with the letters BFC glinting in the morning sun.

"Ah." Boulder seemed to be in his element. Perhaps he secretly wanted to be a law professor, Mark thought. "So you see BFC as the easy life at lower pay?"

"Not at all. I hope that BFC will take away the hours chase, which I found always distracted me from doing the real work. At my old firm, hours, not professional service, was the driving factor."

Boulder nodded.

"But," Mark continued, "to be honest, I'm in a bit of a funk these days. I wasn't sure if it was just my poor experience at my last firm, or the practice of law in general."

"Uh-oh."

"That didn't come out right." Mark quickly added. He struggled with how he could explain to Boulder that if things didn't work out for him at BFC then he would leave law altogether. Things seemed to be completely out of balance at his old firm and he didn't enjoy it. There seemed to be no sense of connection between what he did and what was important to the firm.

"Let me put it this way. Things just didn't feel right at my old firm."

"Things," Boulder murmured, echoing Mark.

"Actually, nothing felt right at my old firm. I needed a fresh approach to my life. And to my career."

Boulder didn't reply. He just nodded his head in sympathetic agreement as they neared the entrance of the BFC building.

"Well then, young Jedi," Boulder grasped Mark firmly around the shoulders. "I believe you are now ready for your BFC training." He opened the door of the BFC building and motioned Mark into the high atrium lobby.

"Hey, Boulder!" A shout came from behind them.

"Omar! How are you on this glorious morning?"

"Excellent, man!" He looked at Mark. "Sorry, didn't know you were with a client."

"Not at all, this is Reynolds, Mark Reynolds—the new guy. Taking over Terry's old spot."

"Nice to meet you, I'm Omar Saud. Part of Stephen's group." He turned to Boulder. "A bit overdressed, isn't he?"

"I already told him."

"You'll like Terry's desk," Saud said to Mark. "They did a great job of cleaning it up. Apparently blood doesn't stick to the seating covers."

"Blood?"

"Boulder didn't tell you?" He winked at Boulder, then continued. "Well, it's nothing really. Terry was a Harvard man from Wall Street and had some—ah—adjustment issues at BFC. Kept insisting on timesheets and always going on about wanting to be more in control of the files." Saud was waving his hands manically, imitating, Mark supposed, the guy who used to sit at Mark's desk. "One day, he just lost it. We came into work and, well, the gun was on the floor beside him." Mark didn't know whether to believe Saud or not. He looked over at Boulder, who had an equally solemn look.

"He'd been lying there for some time. I heard that the time of death was around 9:00 p.m., so of course he was the only one in the shop." Suddenly the solemnity was broken by a look of excitement on Saud's face. "Hey," he said slapping Mark on the shoulder. "You ever seen brain bits after they've hardened? Look like burnt tacos. Crazy. In any event, they clean up well. Don't you worry."

Mark looked back at Boulder, who was doing his best to keep from smiling but failing miserably at it. This little story was clearly their way to initiate the new guy.

"Sorry, mate," Boulder said to Saud. "I couldn't keep it in any longer. It was the part about burnt tacos that got me."

"I must admit that you had me going for a while," Mark said.

"Welcome to BFC, Mark," Saud said. "Tonight we'll take you out for a snipe hunt."

They walked deeper into the lobby of the building, stopping in front of a living wall, next to which stood a large pedestal. On top of the pedestal sat thick, cast-bronze letters:

BFC SELLS RESULTS—NOT TIME

"This used to be a candy warehouse," Boulder said, looking up the living wall to the blue sky above the atrium. "But I suppose that they already told you that when you interviewed. Now, it's a LEED Platinum[7] law firm that runs like clockwork." There was obvious pride in the way he spoke his words. Pride, Mark thought, not based on the size of the deals the firm did, the clients the firm served, or the money the firm made—but pride

---

[7] LEED (Leadership in Energy and Environmental Design) is a third-party certification program for buildings that promotes sustainability and environmental health. There are four levels of certification: certified, silver, gold, and platinum. Platinum is the highest level.

in that the organization worked like clockwork and in its ideals, LEED Platinum. This was something that Mark hadn't expected, something that he hadn't seen at other law firms. Boulder and Saud said their goodbyes leaving Mark to check in with human resources. He noticed that they both reached out to tap the bronze letters as they passed by, Boulder touching the B in BFC, and Saud the T in Time.

Mark announced himself to the receptionist, then sat in the waiting area next to the living wall. A small sign read:

> *This living wall not only cleans our air and provides a pleasing aesthetic for our team, it symbolizes BFC's commitment to leave the world in better shape for our children and our children's children.*

Mark watched staff and lawyers walk past the bronze words. Nearly all of them made a point of touching some part of the words as they passed to the elevators. It was clearly a ritual at BFC, like the rituals of professional sports teams that were meant to bring them luck or success. He also recalled how customers at a national department store had rubbed the toe on a bronze statue of the store's long-dead founder, for luck.

Mark got up and walked over to the letters during a lull in the morning rush. The top of most of the letters were well-worn and shiny. The large B in BFC was clearly getting the worse of it and he could see that the once-sharp edges along the top of the letter were becoming rounded. Mark wondered how many years it would take before they would have to replace it.

"Not to worry," a voice sounded from behind him. "It's not mandatory."

"Sorry?" Mark turned to see a tall woman standing behind him.

"The shining of the words," she continued. "It's not mandatory. Many of the team here touch the top of the words for luck, or as a constant reminder of what it is we do here." She paused for a moment, then, offered an outstretched hand. "Kamilla Awonnahe, I'm the new assistant HR administrator. I think I started just after you interviewed here last. Welcome to BFC."

"Mark Reynolds," he said returning the firm handshake.

She stepped back and gave him a quick once over. Before she could say anything, he jumped in "I know, I know. I'm overdressed."

"I wasn't going to say anything. Your co-workers would do that bit for me. I was just looking at your lapel. Is that—"

Mark cursed himself for grabbing a bite to eat on his way to the office as he tucked his head downward to get a look. Yes, it was a spot of foam from the latte he had picked up before heading to the subway.

"Not to worry, there's a washroom near your desk," she added, motioning him to follow her to her office. "You can sort it out later. It doesn't look too bad. And if you can't get it out, there's a drycleaner around the corner. Most of the lawyers keep a suit in their closet just in case a client wants to meet, so we do a pretty good business with that drycleaner. But, going forward," she said with a smile. "Keep it casual, you'll work better. Now, I have a few forms for you to fill out, then Rachel Nguyen, our senior VP of professional development, will give you a tour and set you up at your desk."

***

Mark was glad that his desk was near a window. The lack of walled offices meant that sunlight streamed through the large warehouse windows to the entire floor, giving pretty much everyone a window seat, but Mark's desk next to the window gave him the ability to see the outside from his chair. There was no need to stand up and look over a privacy wall.

Rachel had finished the office tour, which he enjoyed almost as much as the first time just a month before. BFC didn't feel like a law firm; it had more energy, more liveliness, more youth, and more creativity about it; the color scheme was bright and even playful. The open concept of the office made it feel more social, more connected—like a community. Rachel had said that the BFC office plan was based upon the original designs of Bob Propst, known as the creator of the open-plan office.[8] Unlike the uniform and symmetrical cubicles found in many modern offices, Propst had envisioned offices being designed in a less linear and less uniform manner so that the office would be a "kinetic, active, alert, and vigorous environment." At BFC the office space was a warren of stylized work areas coordinated into what Rachel called work plazas and team neighborhoods.

"Dilbert would be very happy here," Mark had mentioned during the tour.

"That's the idea," Rachel had replied. "This is far from being a cube farm."

Everything about the design made a statement about how BFC was different: the sleek, café-style coffee stations; the gym (with change rooms and showers); the bike parking; the use of recycled components in design features; the lounge areas with flat-screen TVs, foosball and pool tables, and video games—and the main attraction, the rooftop deck overlooking the city.

"We put a lot of effort into office design," Rachel had said during the tour, "because in the studies we reviewed most lawyers and staff said that they work better in a better-designed workspace. They feel motivated, happier, and more willing to be productive and work harder. We want engaged staff and better workflow. We also believe that transparency and openness lead to innovation, so

---

[8] BOB PROPST, THE OFFICE: A FACILITY BASED ON CHANGE (Herman Miller 1968).

we don't like doors – they tend to discourage collaboration and discussion. Our teams are also quite mobile between our hub, the spoke offices, the Philippines, India, and client offices. So we had to rethink how we use all our space to ensure it aligns with how we work and with the values of our workforce. For instance, the generation now joining BFC places a high value on liking the people they work with, so we have created a lunch area that encourages interaction, and we have more boardrooms and more casual meeting spaces as well as quiet areas for work.

"We've had lawyers review and sign documents while on the treadmills. And yoga classes are becoming a huge draw." Rachel had smiled broadly with this comment. "We try hard to give the place a creative-energy type of feel, like you would find in an architect's office or in an advertising office. We want you to want to come to work."

But now it was time to settle into his personal work environment: a half-octagon-shaped pod with desk, shelves, flip-down visitor chair, small closet, and some live plants along the top of the divider. All overhead lighting was specially designed and focused upward, Rachel had said, so that the light reflected upward off the ceiling rather than pounding down on the team, allowing even those who were most sensitive to fluorescent light to work comfortably.

A laptop was perched on a riser located above a pull-out keyboard tray. "The laptop is temporary. We give each of the lawyers a technology payment so that you can go out and purchase your own hardware. It's yours to keep, so choose something that you will enjoy working with. Tablets seem to the choice of late. The same applies to your mobile phone. Buy whichever model you prefer."

Rachel motioned for him to sit down so that she could adjust his posture and seating in front of the computer. "This is your optimal alignment," she said. "See how your arms are bent at 90 degrees and your head is neutral? Your back is supported, right? Keep your feet on the foot rest, or flat on the floor."

"Feels great," Mark replied.

"And take frequent breaks; they'll reduce fatigue. If you feel any pain or have problems, call me immediately and we'll find a solution. We take our workplace environment very seriously and we'll find the right solution for you. When you get your device we can double check the alignments again but at least now you know how your body should be properly aligned at a work station."

Mark appreciated her concern but he was amazed that a senior vice-president would be doing this personally; one of the senior management team taking time to set up the new guy! As odd as it was, it also made him feel important, welcome.

"We believe that relationships with your co-workers are just as important as your online training with your avatar material. You can be the best lawyer in the country but your co-workers are the ones who are going to help you adjust to our workplace. In this case we've assigned you a mentor or 'buddy' who is your go-to person for day-to-day things. Her name is Nancy Kwan. She will have lunch with you every Thursday during your first six months here—all at the expense of BFC. Her annual evaluation will also be based in part upon how she mentored you.

"After two years here you will mentor a newcomer, but first you will have to take the training session—"

"A class?" Mark blurted out.

"Of course," Rachel said. "Mentoring doesn't come naturally to everyone. We take our staff and training very seriously here—it sets us apart, builds our competitive advantage."

"At my last firm," Mark said "they had me fill out HR forms, walked me around the office, introduced me to a bunch of people, then slapped the manual on my desk and that was pretty much it."

"So welcoming—explains why you jumped ship to us."

He smiled. Yes, perhaps it really did start at the welcome, or lack thereof.

"We don't want to lose you over something as easy to get right as orientation. Sylvester Bowen always talks about setting the 'tone' in all things we do in the work place. The tone is our personality and our brand. It's who we are and how we do things. It's not just about setting high standards and relentlessly pursing them—everyone says that. We really do pursue excellence in everything that we do, including the orientation process. We want you to be successful and happy at BFC. We want to create what some call a virtuous circle—with proper support and encouragement, new lawyers become more confident and they take more initiative, which leads to more success, which leads to more encouragement, and so on."

"Seems pretty labor intensive."

"Sure, but we look at the long term—the investment we make now always pays off by creating effective lawyers at a much faster pace than at other firms."

Rachel paused, appearing to consult a mental checklist. "Oh. And don't hesitate to call the masseuse. That's why we pay her—to free up any frozen shoulders."

"That won't be a hard request to follow," Mark responded. Free massages, whenever he needed it? Or rather, whenever he wanted it? Pinch me now, he thought.

"Questions, so far?"

He shook his head as he looked around his workspace. Privacy walls between pods were no more than five feet high, which, when combined with the eleven-foot warehouse ceilings, gave an open, yet private feel.

"Our office layout," Rachel said, noticing his wandering eye, "provides maximum air circulation. Allowing the firm to not only reduce its heating and air-conditioning costs, but also allowing us to regulate the temperature much more effectively." She sounded a little like a bad office brochure, Mark thought, particularly when she began gushing over the special coating on the office's large windows, coating that reduced heat transmission and glare. And she became extremely enthusiastic over the specialty window blinds that automatically lowered, based on the time of day. But she certainly enjoyed her job.

"I don't think that I have to tell you how quickly fights over thermostats can escalate out of control," she continued.

"At my old firm," Mark said, "the guy in the office next to mine had the same body heat as me so it wasn't an issue. But my secretary was so cold that she had a space heater under her desk in the middle of summer."

"It's a common problem that affects productivity and the working environment," Rachel replied. "Not only does that affect the warring parties, but that venomous atmosphere affects the entire workforce. People take sides and it starts to resemble an unruly grade school class. But more importantly, it disrupts work-place rhythm—people constantly adjusting thermostats and focusing on the weather, rather than on the work at hand. They dread coming to the office. Or they start wearing unprofessional clothing that is warm—or cool. It's a much bigger disruption than people think." Mark had to stop himself from staring at her in mild amusement. He couldn't remember anyone at his old firm being this excited about their office space.

"The open-office concept," she continued, "prevents lawyers and executives from hiding away from the firm and pretending that everything is fine. It forces them to be part of the firm; it destroys hierarchy and creates empathy. Then there is the space saving element. Do you know the average size for law offices in this country on a square foot per lawyer basis?"

He shook his head.

"No? Come on. Take a guess." She was smiling and cajoling him to take part in her world.

"Ah, I don't know, 500 square feet?" Mark really had no idea what any amount of square footage per lawyer would look like, and simply spouted out an arbitrary number.

"Nope." She began nodding her head, smiling and waving her hands in a motion meant to give him a second chance to guess the right answer.

It was his first day at the office and he didn't want to offend anyone. So he played along. "Hmm, 750?" he suggested with the most perplexed expression he could muster in order for her to stop what he considered to be a very silly game.

"Close! It's anywhere from 800 to 900 square feet per lawyer."[9]

"Wow!" he said mustering forced enthusiasm even though he had not the faintest clue what the numbers meant. But clearly "800–900" was a number that was meant to overwhelm him.

"But at this location of BFC," she said, "we have taken that down to 300 square feet."

"Oh!" he said, genuinely impressed that BFC used only a third of the office space used by most other firms. "That must save a ton of money on overhead."

She nodded. "The cost savings pretty much shut down any debate over private offices. But it's more than that. When a firm breaks down walls and creates open office space, it puts everyone on the same level. You've already seen that there are no corner offices, that no one's workspace is any larger than anyone else's. All of which flows into our model that everyone is important at BFC and that everyone's contribution is important to our overall

---

[9] Knoll Workplace Research recommends between 650 to 1,000 sf per lawyer when planning a new office. *See*, "The Emerging Law Firm Practice," 2009, page 3.

success. It creates a feeling of community, a feeling that no one is better than anyone else."

Mark agreed. What she was saying made a lot of sense. Creating equality among all meant that the petty jealousies that he had seen at his previous firm would never have a chance to develop here.

"What if I need a private meeting?"

"There are a number of smaller meeting rooms throughout the building that you can book. Don't be put off by the open concept. You'll soon find that having a private office is actually a bad idea—it stifles teamwork—and that the number of private meetings that you really need are quite few." She paused before beginning a new thought.

"Our firm keeps a youthful feel about it, so we focus on other things, like the color schemes, for example. Vibrant and youthful, don't you think?"

"Yes, and the rooftop deck is fantastic," Mark said. "It completely sold me on the firm."

"I hear that a lot—especially from clients when we have firm functions up there. But you're right. Every little bit helps boost firm morale; like our dress code being permanently business-casual."

She walked closer to the laptop, then added, "Lawyers who are excessively self-interested don't do well here. Nor do the ones that need the material trappings of law." She noticed that Mark looked perplexed at her "trappings of law" comment, and expanded: "The separate office, mahogany desk, client table and chair, wall space for all your university degrees."

He nodded his understanding.

To drive home the point more firmly, she added, "If a lawyer needs those items in order to work—then he became a lawyer for all the wrong reasons."

Rachel helped him log into his laptop to verify that he was properly set up, not only with the computer itself, but with the wi-fi system; BFC did not run any cabling in the office. "Less expense and reduces the need for in-house technical people," Rachel said switching on his laptop. "In fact, we have no IT people."

"But what if I have a software problem or a network problem?" Mark was taken aback that there was no one to help with technical problems.

"If you have a problem dial 979 and our outsourced personnel will handle it." She smiled. "Part of the beauty of working in the cloud and with SaaS."

She saw a puzzled look on Mark's face. "SaaS stands for 'software as a service.' Software is not installed on our machines; we access it through the cloud. It eliminates the need for IT staff in-house and that keeps us at the forefront of cost reduction and reduces down time. No need to buy upgrades and install them. The software is constantly upgraded under the terms of our contract with the service provider."

"Got it," Mark replied.

"The 'cloud' is simply a huge collection of servers operated by third parties in a remote location. All e-mails and documents are located in the cloud and are accessible by anyone in the firm from anywhere in the world. Since everything is in the cloud, we don't store data on site, or in our computers where it is susceptible to damage or destruction by fire, or theft if a lawyer has a computer stolen or she loses a USB key with data on it. It saves us money in power consumption and cooling costs, and saves space. We can scale up or down quickly when we need more IT capacity and it allows us to work from any place there is Internet access."

"Hold on," Mark said. "Don't we have some ethical and confidentiality issues putting our data in the hands of third parties?" He was alarmed by this prospect.

"Good question. It's one that we get often."

Rachel pulled the flip-down visitor's chair and sat across from Mark.

"First, the data remains our property, not that of the cloud provider. It's fully encrypted and we own and control the encryption keys. Our ethical obligations are satisfied as long as we take reasonable care to minimize the risks to loss of confidentiality and loss of client information. We are not required to guarantee that the system will be infallibly secure. No law firm is."

"But isn't it safer on site?"

"Another good question. Let me answer it this way. The cloud provider's core business is to maintain a secure environment with maximum uptime. That is not BFC's core business. So how can we realistically say that BFC can provide a more secure and better IT solution? Let me also suggest to you that a law firm's greatest security risks come from its own staff, either accidently, as I mentioned before with lost USB keys—or deliberately."

"I suppose that you've done all your due diligence on the cloud provider, where the data is held, and set up appropriate service-level agreements?"

"Absolutely."

"And all clients know that their data is held in the cloud?"

"Correct. And they explicitly agree to it in writing."

"Wow. Sounds great," Mark replied.

"It also allows for ease of access by our secretarial staff here and our night secretarial staff in Manila."

"We have night staff in the Philippines?"

"Sure, why not? Do you realize how expensive it is to hire night secretaries? It's much better to have staff in a low-cost environment working during their normal daylight hours."

"But what if I have to speak to them about something? How do—"

Rachel put up her hand. "We'll get there. Now, watch the screen."

The laptop screen glowed with the standard software operating system logo before adding a cheery welcome:

GOOD MORNING, MARK!

"Pretty standard fare," Rachel said. "I imagine that your previous firm had a similar sort of welcome. But next up, you will see the BFC mantra pop up. Right about now."

On cue the screen changed.

BFC PERFORMS:

Legal services that differ from those of our rivals
or
Similar legal services, but in a very different way[10]

After these two messages, another window popped up, but, Rachel told him, only at the first log-in. That window showed a photograph of a BFC employee with the caption:

How well do you know this BFC colleague?[11]

Below the caption were a number of answers to choose from:

---

[10] BFC borrowed this phrasing from Michael Porter, *What is Strategy?*, HARV. BUS. REV., Nov.–Dec. 1996. Porter argues that there is a difference between operational effectiveness and strategy. Operational effectiveness is a necessary part of each company or in this case, law firm, but it is not in itself, a strategy for the firm. That is why BFC does not see any of its initiatives, such as BFSigma and legal project management, as anything more than tools to be used to differentiate itself from other legal services providers. BFC's real competitive advantage is being different from other providers.

[11] This concept was utilized by Zappos.com to improve company-wide congeniality. *See* Tony Hsieh, *Why I Sold Zappos,* INC., June 1, 2010, http://preview.inc.com/magazine/20100601/why-i-sold-zappos_pagen_2.html.

- I've never seen this person before
- We say "hi" in the halls
- We hang out during work hours
- We hang out outside of work
- We're going to be long-time friends

Noting Mark's reaction, a reaction that clearly said *Wow! That's intrusive*, Rachel explained. "The purpose of this is to break down silos and foster congeniality among everyone at the firm. At BFC we are stronger if we work across departments. There is nothing worse than having a firm social event and seeing people grouped only among their work departments. Our strength comes from truly being one firm across all areas of law."

Rachel clicked the box beside the phrase "I've never seen this person before." The screen changed to a standard desktop configuration. Looking back at Mark she could still see his eyes register serious concern. "Relax! There is no right or wrong answer. The data is blind to the specific respondent, but it's coordinated by practice area and location within the firm. It also gives us a sense of traffic patterns, which helps us determine if we need to redesign our work areas to accommodate those traffic patterns. One of our lawyers got the idea from one of our Internet clients and Bowen loved it. It works on the theory that the more people you know and the more you interconnect with them, the better ideas we will come up with that fulfill our mantra of doing different activities, or doing similar activities differently."

Mark wasn't the shyest lawyer at his old firm, but meeting new people was a continuing challenge for him. It was a skill that he had not completely mastered.

"And not to worry, we have a class for that!" Rachel added.

"A class for what?"

"A class on interaction within the firm and with clients."

"You're kidding me, right?"

"Not at all. The course is a very useful one and is designed to give you tools that everyone assumes that they are born with, social ability. It provides a list of potential ice-breakers; pointers on how to properly introduce yourself, the firm, and other colleagues to clients and others; and how to work a room. The purpose is to give each lawyer the social tools necessary to succeed at BFC and also to deal with clients effectively."

"Sure," Mark said, already planning a plausible excuse not to attend.

"I get that response from all the newbies. But I assure you, everyone who takes the program is astounded by how helpful it is. Especially the video."

"Video?"

"There is no better way to show how you appear to clients and others than by video." She ignored his look of terror and continued on. "Oh, and, just in case you're planning a pass on the course, I will tell you that it is mandatory and will be part of your annual evaluation."

Mark smiled, gritting his teeth.

Rachel continued on. "Sylvester Bowen maintains his Breakfast with Bowen program, in which he sits down with small groups of five employees, selected at random, for breakfast every week. We host that in the lunch area or sometimes he takes it off-site. He likes to make sure that he has the pulse of the firm and that everyone feels as if they can make a contribution, and speak directly to him."

She took the mouse for the laptop and clicked on the contacts folder. "Watch this." The laptop's built-in webcam turned on and Mark could see himself and Rachel on the monitor. Rachel clicked on a new icon and soon a phone ringtone could be heard through the laptop speakers.

"Normally, you would be wearing a headset so that you won't be too noisy, or you could take this to a boardroom. But this will work for now."

"Hullo?" A voice was heard through the speakers and a woman wearing a headset appeared onscreen.

"Joanne, hi! Can you see us? It's Rachel Nguyen and our new recruit, Mark Reynolds." Joanne was one of BFC's local home-sourcers; a lawyer who worked from her home and helped with project matters from time to time on a piecework basis. She embodied BFC's just-in-time capacity to aid with overflow and normal course work. Joanne had worked at BFC some years ago but wanted to spend more time as a stay-at-home mom.

The home-sourcing program, Rachel explained, was a win/win: BFC keeps valued lawyers and the lawyers keep a modicum of practice.

"Now I know the answer to my question about night staffing in Manila," Mark said.

"Exactly," Rachel affirmed. "All our overseas staff are on the contact list and you will be able to speak to them via our voice-over-IP system and see them via webcam. You will have no difficulty communicating your needs to them. We also have an instant messaging system that lets you communicate that way, if you prefer."

"It connects to India as well?" Mark asked.

"India, within this office, and even with some of our clients," Rachel said. "More and more clients are asking for instant messaging to our lawyers. Greater connectivity promotes a closer bond between clients and the firm—which is never a bad thing."

She waved to Joanne on the webcam. "Thanks for the demo, Jo. Take care." Rachel clicked the mouse again to turn off the webcam and then turned to Mark.

"Our somewhat virtual nature makes us innovative and efficient and saves us money. But it also means that we have to constantly make an effort to create interaction among our team members to promote team building, whether that is through social engagements or regular meetings. Trust needs to be constantly built among our team members. One of our more popular events are the Power Meetings. They're held monthly in the atrium—the only place we can hold everyone comfortably. Everyone is invited and everyone comes unless there's another pressing engagement."

Mark looked skeptical.

"Mark, bear with me here," Rachel said. "Everyone feels weird at first. We are so different from every other firm that you are having a very natural reaction."

Mark tried to keep an open mind.

"What you will find is that the way that law firms traditionally operate is actually far more weird than BFC. We operate like some of the most successful companies in the world. How we operate is actually the norm. What's that saying? 'A rational person seems insane to a room full of psychotics.'"

"I hear you," Mark said. "What happens at the Power Meetings?"

"Sylvester and some of the other executives use this time to make firm announcements and take questions. It is a no holds-barred affair; all questions are answered and all comments from the floor are respected. We also ensure that the meetings are broadcast live to our people in India and the Philippines. We also include our home-sourcers.

"We need to constantly reinforce a sense of ownership and membership within the firm. The time difference is a challenge but we try our best to set the meetings at times that are not outrageous, and videos of the meetings are always available. The culture we promote at BFC is one of openness and transparency where everyone is valuable to BFC. It's why we have temporary assignments to the legal process outsourcing group in India and to the knowledge management group in Manila; they create a steady stream of connections with what some say are the far-flung elements of the BFC empire."

She pulled some papers from her binder. "Your training schedule is all sorted out here, it's also in your electric calendar." She placed a month's-view calendar on the desk. "Don't make too many plans for this month; you've got a lot to catch up on. We do things very differently at BFC."

Her cell phone rang. She looked at the screen and frowned.

"Sorry, gotta take this. It'll just be a moment. Take a look at your schedule and let me know if you have any questions." Rachel walked a few steps away from Mark and began speaking into the phone.

Mark picked up the calendar. All meetings were color-coded so that he could see how they matched up for weeks. Budgeting skills were in purple. Value-based billing techniques in blue. Legal project management training took up much of next week, followed by legal process outsourcing via voice-over-IP in the training room. Another set of training was called BFSigma,[12] which Rachel had previously told him was a bastardized six sigma or lean six sigma training in which BFC had invested heavily to make the firm more efficient in the way it handled files, created benchmarks, and got client feedback. This was vital as it allowed the firm to set fees more reliably and predictably on all matters. "BFC was of the view," she had said during their tour, "that the more time that lawyers spent thinking about what they were doing and why they were doing it, the better the firm could reliably and profitably set fees." A little note at the bottom of the calendar reminded him to arrange for his one-month assignment

---

[12] The purpose of BFSigma is to eliminate wasteful steps in any legal work being performed.

to India to work with the LPO team followed by his assignment to Manila.

"Sorry about that," Rachel was off the phone now. "Teenage daughter crisis. Now, where was I?"

"You were planning the rest of my life," Mark said with a smile.

"Wait until you see next month," she said.

"And before you even mention it," she added. "You are fully able to work from your home as needed. However, I caution you, as I caution all the lawyers who start here, there is a reason why the good Lord created offices. At one point in time it was necessary for everything to be done in a centralized environment—before the Internet, cloud computing, cell phones, e-mail, and texting. What was taken for granted at that time was the sense of community that one got from working together in one location.

"Whether we choose to admit it or not, a law firm is a social organization, with everyone in it looking for a sense of community, a sense of belonging, and a sense of support. But you don't have to take my word for it. Stephen Mayson said, 'People's response to an organization will be shaped by their perception of themselves, their perceptions of others, their roles, the way in which power and influence are used, and its culture.'[13] There is little that we can do to shape people's perception of themselves and others, but we can address the third-party elements, how their roles are perceived by BFC and the way that power and influence are used at BFC."

"I agree, but there also has to be a motivation factor, like money or prestige," Mark replied.

"Perhaps, but people—including lawyers—will also respond positively to effective leadership, appraisal, and training and development.[14] That's what we concentrate on here. Actually,

---

[13] Stephen Mayson, Making Sense of Law Firms 529.

[14] *Id.*

let me state that a different way: we believe that money does not buy loyalty. What does create loyalty is effective leadership, fair and transparent appraisals and compensation, challenging and interesting work, and a focus on training and development. We spend a great deal of effort creating a connection to the firm, making sure that the team feels their work has meaning and that they are valued by BFC. And most important, that we maintain some sense of fun. As you know, any new lawyer who feels she can't fit in with our culture during her first year can request a release, with no questions asked – along with a termination bonus."

"How many have been released?" Mark asked.

"Very few, in fact no one in the last five years has asked for a release. But enough of the infomercial. Any successful office, virtual or real, needs a focal point or home base to solidify the feeling of community, which is why I encourage you to work from the sat office as much as possible." She paused before continuing. "For many, myself included, the distractions in a home environment are too great. In fact, I'm far less productive at home than I am at work—and I live alone. Having the ability to call someone on the phone or see them via a webcam does not fulfill my very human need to work together in close proximity in a community. The home-sourcers relish the opportunity to come into the office for a meeting of some kind so that they can tap into our community."

"Nothing to worry about here," Mark replied. "I have two young children. Work is impossible in that environment. And it's also nice to go somewhere else for each part of your life. I have friends who are freelance writers and work out of the home, probably less efficiently as you say, but they uniformly all say that they're lonely and miss interacting with people, even though they're on the phone constantly with interviews and their editors. There's something about being among others that's important to us."

"But it's more than that," Rachel continued. "I believe that our brains are wired to work in certain environments, to sleep in certain environments, to play and to eat in others. If you do all these functions in the same environment, your brain becomes confused and less able to focus on the task at hand because it recalls all the other activities that you do in that space, causing distraction."

Rachel leaned against Mark's desk to rest for a moment.

"You'll also notice that there is no such thing as a timesheet here. All our fees are all value-based. Bowen is fond of saying that any law firm that focuses on maximizing billable hours will become obsolete."

"What's his rationale behind that?"

"You'll have to ask him, but my take is that a focus on billable hours inhibits any innovation that would reduce costs to a client, since reducing client costs runs counter to the notion of maximizing billable hours. And if your business model is built on maximizing billable hours, then you can never save client costs and you are vulnerable to any provider that reduces those costs. But worse still, you have no ability to react to such a provider because your business model does not allow you to do so."

Mark nodded thoughtfully.

"Nor do we track most disbursements," Rachel added. "We view administrative time as valuable time. Time used tracking fax charges, long distance charges, or courier charges is time that could be better spent somewhere else. Recovering out-of-pocket expenses at the cost of staff and attorney time makes no sense to us."

"Like McLuhan said, first we shape our tools, then our tools shape us," Mark said.

"Exactly. The tools of lawyers—billable hours and recaptured disbursements—now threaten to shape lawyers into obsolete creatures. Which is why, if BFC is to continue to be successful, it has to be built on a different model of behavior. But I'll leave BFC philosophy to Sylvester." She pushed away from the desk satisfied that she had said enough for the day—perhaps too much for Mark to absorb.

"Also," she added. "You have a passport, right?"

Mark nodded.

"Bring it in when you get a chance so that we can get your visa application sorted out for India. Every lawyer does a temporary assignment at our LPO; it gives you a chance to understand its capabilities and operations so that you can better utilize it in your day-to-day practice. And again, it builds community. As part of that trip, you'll also pop into our knowledge management operations in Manila. Barry will tell you more about that operation when he arrives tomorrow morning.

"Let me leave you with a few words on your annual evaluation. It will take into account many things in determining your success at BFC. Certainly the usual suspects of professional competence, and how you get along with the others in the firm and with clients, are graded. But we go much deeper here at BFC.

"Your evaluation will also review how well you follow firm policy, firm style in document preparation, knowledge management contribution, and your professional development as a whole, including self-identification of areas you need to learn better. I know this is counterintuitive for lawyers, but at BFC we want to know, and we want you to acknowledge, those areas where you need to improve. You'll be reviewed on improvement in those areas. You become a better lawyer, and BFC gets better as a result.

"Now, if there aren't any more questions, I'll leave you to take some time with your avatar training and to review the BFC bible," she said looking toward his bookshelf. It was empty.

"It's not here! Damn!"

She turned back to Mark. "I'm sorry about that. It was supposed to be sent over this morning. Let me look into that and get it sent to you straight away. In the meantime, take a look at our paperless office procedures; they're online. We don't like paper here—except for the bible. Scan it, then can it."

"Catchy phrase," Mark murmured to himself.

CHAPTER 5
Avatars and KM

Mark came in early the next morning to continue his BFC online training. He thought that the avatar concept was silly at first, but soon warmed to it.

He clicked the training icon on his laptop. The screen gave him a number of modules to select. He decided to start with BFC e-mail policy.

The screen changed to a computer-generated rendering of a rooftop in a large city. He had entered a virtual world and his avatar was waiting for him. He maneuvered the avatar across the rooftop toward another avatar who was the instructor for the lesson. This was e-learning by gaming; a videogame merged with education, Rachel had told him. BFC had devised a number of training modules in which employees would watch avatars interact as a method of displaying the lesson to be learned. There was a test after each lesson; a participant who answered the questions correctly would gain points and move on to the next level in the "game."

"It makes learning much more fun," Rachel had said yesterday. "A well-designed game experience is far superior and more cost-effective for training team members—it makes them better able to retain information and they pay more attention because of the fun element. It also allows us to put lawyers and staff into actual client situations. When players are rewarded or punished based on their actions, they receive immediate feedback so they can fix a mistake. It also allows us in human resources to see how the team member is doing and to ensure that she has completed her training."

"It's learning by doing," Mark had said, "just virtually."

"Right, and isn't that the best teaching approach?"

"I can see a lot of younger lawyers and staff enjoying this," Mark had said "Our generation is more of a gaming generation."

"That's why we do it," she had said. "We wanted something that would resonate. But there are also good business reasons behind it." She had looked at Mark for his thoughts.

"It saves you the hassle of finding people to give seminars and we can learn on our own time," he had replied.

"Correct. It also provides a consistent message and it's flexible enough to cross cultures and languages. For instance, we can send the same game to India or to the Philippines or any other country where we have operations, and simply change the language soundtrack and the appearance of the avatars to reflect the people in that office. We don't have to send a trainer and the message stays consistent across offices.

"All our training, whether it is on firm policy or legal issues, is now done in this format. The gaming aspect makes people want to learn so that they can get to the next level. People are challenged by that and I often hear discussions over what levels people have attained and how fast they attained it."

"I suppose you can also create modules and sell them to clients anywhere in the world for training," Mark had said.

"And we do," she had replied. "Last month we acted for a Chinese company in making a large corporate acquisition here. The executives from China who were sent to oversee the acquisition needed training on local labor and employment practices. We changed the sound track to Mandarin and modified the avatars on our standard employment and labor law video—and yes, we took out the gaming part for them." She had smiled. "Training videos have now become a profit center for BFC."

Mark shook his head to refocus on the module he was now starting; BFC e-mail policy didn't seem to be too difficult to master. The policy is not a usage policy, the lead avatar explained; it's an efficiency tool that all staff and lawyers need to master in order to make themselves more efficient. All BFC personnel were to carefully think about every e-mail they send to consider how the reader will read it, what message the e-mail conveyed, and whether the e-mail would be easily understood. It is the responsibility of the sender to ensure that the person reading the e-mail can quickly understand the message. An e-mail that has the recipient scratching her head is wasted time. This includes preparing the appropriate subject line, so the recipient knows exactly what the e-mail is about. The avatar continued with a number of small vignettes to illustrate a number of e-mail policy matters.

When the lead avatar had finished speaking, Mark moved his avatar across the rooftop to the challenge portion of the module. In this case it was a series of hurdles that his avatar would have to jump over before Mark could move to the next training level. But in order to gain enough strength to jump over each hurdle, Mark had to correctly answer a test question located in front of each hurdle.

He maneuvered his avatar to the first question. It was about the content of e-mail messages. Mark selected the answer, "Brevity is best." His avatar puffed out its chest and seemed to grow slightly before running toward the hurdle and leaping over it. He had gotten the first question correct.

Before him lay the next hurdle and a question about the meaning of "NNTR." He selected the answer "No need to reply." Again his avatar puffed out his chest, grew slightly, and cleared the hurdle.

On it went for eight more hurdles, with correct answers allowing his avatar to clear the hurdle and a wrong answer making the avatar run straight into the hurdle without a leap. Mark suppressed the urge to deliberately get an answer wrong and make his avatar smash head-on into a hurdle, for the sheer fun of it. He had already tried, and failed, to make his avatar jump off the rooftop.

When Mark cleared the final hurdle, he checked his watch. He still had some time before Barry Spunker, senior vice president for knowledge management, was to arrive to give Mark his tour, but not quite enough time to start another avatar module. Mark pulled the BFC bible from his bookshelf. The bible was deliberated printed and bound, Rachel had told him. It reinforced the permanence of the firm and reiterated the importance of its contents. Its cover was filled with scrolling characters reminiscent of ancient runes. Cute, he thought. They really take things seriously here. Not that that was a bad thing. Just unusual for a firm to live and breathe its values.

Mark paged through the table of contents. The binder was filled with articles prepared by senior members of the firm about things that they had learned and wished to pass on to the next generation. There was the expected piece on the history of the firm by Bowen, followed by articles from others in the firm that spoke to things as mundane as asking for guidance from senior people and dealing with cross-cultural differences in the firm's legal processing outsourcing in Mumbai and the knowledge management personnel in Philippines. Mark was reading a short article on the proper use of the Tagalog word "po" as a show of respect, when Spunker arrived.

Barry Spunker seemed to be the antithesis of a law firm knowledge management director; his rapid-clip manner of speech, coupled with disheveled dress and hair suggested that he was more mad scientist than Big Law lawyer, or perhaps a cross between a mad scientist and bassist for an 1980s rock band.

Spunker had quit the formal practice of law over fifteen years ago and, in his words, "devoted" himself to knowledge management long before it was fashionable—if, Mark thought, one could consider it to be fashionable now. He had spent several years in Sydney and London, where knowledge management was a big-budget item, and was taken very seriously by the top-tier firms.

"Now, what I'm about to show you is our secret sauce," he said, his eyes flashing with glee. "Our secret formula governs the way that BFC works and determines to a very large extent its profitability. Without it, our efficiency and our effectiveness drop to zero and with them go our clients." He ushered Mark into a large, circular area on the third floor of the BFC building. The walls did not rise above eight feet, allowing air flow and light into the room but still providing privacy and quiet for the team. Several BFC staff members were working in front of oversized computer monitors. Each was wearing a head set. Mark looked around, trying to act impressed.

"Well? What do you think?" Spunker said to him. "Is this not the greatest thing you have ever witnessed?"

Mark paused and then turned to Spunker. "I'm sorry, but what is it I'm witnessing?"

"What are you witnessing? Why my boy, this is the sleekest knowledge management system you have ever seen. And it's precisely what you don't see that makes it so wonderful."

Mark's face told Spunker that he was completely lost.

"After all—do you see knowledge? Or is it something that can be called upon when needed, then have it recede into memory for use again later?"

"Sure, I guess," Mark replied.

"You guess? Knowledge should not clutter and one should not know that it is even there. Right? When you learn something in life or in school, that information is processed and then saved somewhere in the recesses of your mind. Am I right?"

Mark nodded.

"But at the typical law firm that information is more often than not lost right after the matter is completed, or it travels to another firm with a lawyer when she leaves, or even worse, it sits idle on a server somewhere where no one will ever find it; the so-called knowledge landfill.[15] A tremendous loss! And so disrespectful to the lawyer who worked hard to create it!"

Spunker's face fell as he spoke, as if in that moment he felt the pain of the situation he had just described. He looked back at Mark.

"I have come to believe," he continued, "that we must think of our work product as works of art. They are to be maintained. Savored. And even polished over time. They are timeless, priceless gems that should be protected, yet also be available for use by the entire firm, and by our clients, at any time."

No lawyer would honestly doubt what Spunker was saying, Mark thought. Precedent documents were vital to the success of a law practice. His old firm had believed that as well. But what exactly was so special about what BFC had? There was nothing revolutionary in the concept of precedent documents being important.

"Now," Spunker continued, "we come to the good part. The radical part. How do you ensure that the firm has accessible well-crafted precedents on everything?" He looked expectedly at Mark and moved his head forward, waiting for a response.

---

[15] I give a great deal of thanks to Matthew Parsons for his superb work, *Effective Knowledge Management for Law Firms, w*hich helped formulate the thoughts in this chapter. Parsons refers to the information landfill on page 78 of his book.

"Well, at my old firm, we had a very cute former associate who would send e-mails requesting precedents every so often so that she could dump them into whatever software she had convinced the firm to buy."

"Ah, an interesting choice of words." Spunker stroked his chin and stared into the ceiling as he rolled the words in his mouth. "Former associate. E-mails. Requests. Dump." He looked back at Mark. "And how did that system, if I might be so bold as to call it a 'system,' work for you?"

"It was all right, I guess."

"Just all right?"

"Well, to be honest," Mark said.

"Honesty is good," Spunker replied.

"I found it confusing and so I just defaulted to my own set of precedents."

"Confusing is bad," Spunker said. "Any other issues?"

"Honestly?"

"Yes, yes, I said honesty is good. We need that at BFC. We thrive on it."

"Well," Mark began. "I was afraid to share my precedents with other lawyers, just in case they thought mine were useless."

"Ah, there was fear of ridicule."

"Yes."

"And so the system broke down."

"You could say that."

"Yes! And I did! And that is exactly where the BFC knowledge management model began. We looked at where the process breaks down, starting from who manages the system. You said that the person in charge was a cute former associate."

Mark nodded. "Very cute."

Spunker gave Mark an odd look. "I'm not sure what her looks have to do with anything, but being a former associate, or an associate about to leave or be fired, is not a good bit of experience for this role. No, not at all. Knowledge management is too important to be seen as a place to put a lawyer out to pasture. It is not a lifestyle choice. It is the life blood of the firm! How the KM director deals with KM affects the entire firm! A good director makes all the difference. He lives and breathes KM, always searching for better ways to manage matters, for ways to make things easier for the firm. Now you can see why I am on the executive team of BFC. But it is more than my sparkling personality."

Spunker took a breath. "How does one ensure," he asked, "that the importance of KM filters down to all in the firm? How effective were her e-mails?"

"A little."

"Exactly. There was always an excuse, wasn't there? Always a reason why documents couldn't be sent off to the KM director."

"Pretty much."

"That's why BFC does something very different. Some have called it dictatorial—ha!—but it works mind you. Dictators have their role, they make things work! And at BFC, it works quite well. Rachel will have told you, or will tell you shortly about annual reviews."

"Yes, done."

"Well—nothing new and exciting there. All firms do them in some sort of fashion, some better than others. Most however, do a very poor job. But you will notice that one of the criteria on your annual review—and the annual review of every lawyer at all levels—is contribution to KM."

He noticed a look of surprise on Mark's face.

"Yes, you will be reviewed on your contributions. The yardstick, however, is not how well-drafted your documents are—there is already an expectation that you draft high-quality documents—but even if you don't, that is not the purpose of KM. Rather, the purpose and the way to score well on that part of your evaluation is to routinely submit documents, memos, opinions and so on to the KM team.

"We are one of the few firms that believe that KM is not an IT solution. There are all kinds of software salespeople out there who will sell you off-the-shelf KM solutions to your needs. And to some extent, software is an important component of a firm's KM strategy. But it is just that—a component. Software is not the strategy and it is not the process, no more than buying a crane is all that is needed to build an office tower." Barry paused to gather his thoughts. "Now getting back to your evaluation, when I say routine, it is because if you wish to be successful at BFC, it will become second nature for you to submit these items to the KM team. KM needs to be fresh, to be kept current. You will not be shy about your prose or punctuation. In fact, you will lie awake sleepless at night if you have somehow forgotten to make even the smallest submission. Because it is only when KM becomes an integral part of your professional life that KM, you, and BFC will succeed."

Mark could not imagine being sleepless over documents, but he supposed that it was possible—particularly if his annual review depended upon it. He thought back to his old firm and the hodge-podge way in which KM was handled. Perhaps the secret to success was tying KM into annual reviews and making it an obligation of each lawyer. His personal experience had shown that making KM contributions an optional part of work in a law firm did not work well.

"After you finish a file," Spunker continued, "typically a transaction, you will have a post-project review session with your team members. Aside from reviewing what was done well and what can be done better, you will then capture KM and send documentation to my team here." A broad smile lit up his face. "We're also doing something that no other firm does, at least to my knowledge: we store agreements by law firm."[16]

"I don't understand," Mark said.

"Sorry, I mean by your adversary on a matter. In other words, we are now able to determine what every major law firm in the city and the country will allow in an agreement and what it won't. It's an important negotiating tool for you to use when you come up against a lawyer who says 'At Simmons LLP we never give that change.' You simply point out the twenty-three other deals in which his firm did give that change."

"Wow. That certainly does drive home the value of KM," Mark said.

"KM also has an integral role in reducing BFC's risk and makes everyone here better at their jobs. KM is behavior and process married together in happily wedded bliss." Spunker seemed pleased with this statement. "Matthew Parsons was absolutely right when he said that a good KM strategy recognizes that KM has three roles to play: first, it is the custodian of the firm's knowledge; second, it is a collector of all new knowledge; and third, it is, for lack of a better word, an 'improver.' KM should be able to demonstrably and measurably improve the firm's performance and profits."[17]

Looking at the small room, Mark asked, "If over 200 lawyers are sending documents every day or so, how is it that you keep up? You must be snowed under with paper."

"Yes, one would think so. Yet here we are." Spunker waved his hands around the room. "Notice any paper piles?"

"None," Mark replied.

---

[16] Pam Woldow mentions this concept in her blog *At the Intersection*.
[17] MATTHEW PARSONS, EFFECTIVE KNOWLEDGE MANAGEMENT FOR LAW FIRMS 27.

"And that of course is another reason why the old model of hiring a pretty lawyer to dump things into a software system does not work. IT and servers are nothing more than tools to be used in the proper fashion. Before we go off and spend hundreds of thousands of dollars—and just to tell you, our annual KM budget is well over $1 million—there needs to be a performance pay-off. As I have said before, a firm must completely buy into KM as an important and vital element of its success. And if does so, it will invest the necessary resources to create and maintain such a system. At BFC, I have the complete and absolute support of the entire executive team to do whatever is necessary to ensure that our KM systems are best in class. And I can tell you from working at other firms, that that tone at the top is vital for success."

Mark continued to look about the room. It was spartan, except for the team working on some sort of documentation that he presumed were KM reports.

"What you don't see," Spunker added, "is the mountain of people that should be vetting and sorting, am I right?"

Mark nodded.

"They do in fact exist. Just not here."

"I can see that."

"There are some good reasons for that. First, when typically would you believe that most lawyers send their documents to the KM team? At the end of the day, correct?"

Mark nodded.

"So, from that standpoint, you need a night crew to sort them. It's very hard to get people who want to work all night, especially lawyers. People prefer to sleep at night, not work. That's why our KM team is in the Philippines. Which as you know from school is on the opposite side of the world. Which means that they sleep when we are awake, and they are awake when we sleep. The documents go out to them each evening from here and they spend their daytime hours sorting them while we sleep. When I arrive in the morning, I have their report on the night's activities."

"What exactly do they do?" Mark asked.

"They are all trained lawyers so they understand the mechanics of legal documentation. They don't have to understand the documents—although I dare say that they probably understand them better than some of our lawyers—they simply review the documents to determine if that document already exists in the system or if an additional clause should be added to the firm's precedents or if a memo on a certain area of law is to be added or deleted. A report is then prepared for the practice heads to review in the morning about changes that are suggested to the current crop of documents. Practice heads then review those changes and determine if they are to be added or not."

"I see," said Mark. It made perfect sense.

"What this accomplishes is not only a system of checks and balances on many levels, but it also ensures that documents are submitted regularly and vetted regularly. A BFC lawyer's success also depends on her review of the document changes and the implementation of those changes. But at the same time, the precedents themselves are policed by our lawyers here to ensure that they are proper and valid."

"Do I send my legal research to the Philippines as well?"

"No. In fact you will do very little research. Most, if not all of our legal research is actually done in India, not the Philippines, through our legal process outsourcing group in Mumbai. It is a logical tie and fits with their mandate to provide legal services. They have some bright lawyers there who love to research and can pull things together much faster than lawyers here. And given the cost of living and salary expectations in India, BFC realizes significant cost savings."

Mark did not complain. He hated conducting legal research and was quite happy to have someone do it for him and send it back to him for review and comments. He did have some concerns over the use of LPOs, particularly since they were located on the other side of the world.

"Barry, have we addressed the ethical issues of using LPOs?"

"Of course! If you look at what law associations and societies have been saying across the world, there are several areas that need to be addressed in order for any lawyer to use an LPO. First, there must be proper, direct, and meaningful supervision of the LPO. As you may know, one of our founding partners, Kamran Chandri, spends most of his time there and we are always rotating lawyers in and out of the facility. We also ensure that the LPO maintains client confidentiality and avoids any conflicts of interest. Most importantly, our clients are all fully aware of our practice and we ensure that the fees billed for work done by the LPO is appropriate in all circumstances."

Mark was speechless. BFC had neatly addressed the main arguments against using LPOs, so it seemed to Mark that the main reason other firms were reluctant to use LPOs was merely a fear of change.

Spunker, however, had moved on in his thinking. "Believe it or not," he said, "though you don't seem to be one of those who would be swayed by this, but we have had a number of lawyers come to us because of our KM system. So inadvertently KM becomes a tool for luring talent to BFC."

Mark raised his eyebrows. "Really?"

"I see the skepticism on your face," Spunker replied. "But it's true. We've had four or five lawyers come to us because they want a more efficient and cutting-edge work space. After all, between you and me, law firms are all the same. Same deals, same work, same money to a certain extent. So what is left to differentiate them in the hunt for talented people? Better systems! Or as I like to say, systems that really work. Think of all the bright minds going to waste and all the new thoughts that run aground simply because they are locked in a firm that doesn't care about its systems and processes.

"Consider if you are an engineer. Would you like to work in a place using super-fast computers or one using slide rulers? As facetious as that sounds, that really is the comparison. Can you still work using slide rulers? Yes, of course. Aren't you able to work better, faster, and more efficiently with a computer, though? And really, what is it that we are selling to our clients? Our good looks and shiny offices? No! Our ability to print out reams of paper? No! We're selling our ability to manipulate information in a way that assists our clients! Remember the bronze words in the lobby downstairs?"

"We sell results, not time," Mark replied.

"Right! I think that you will find that you will become far more efficient because of our KM system and therefore a much happier lawyer."

Spunker paused, then added, "BFC cares about your happiness because being happy makes you a better and more productive worker. Unhappy workers are not productive. Lawyers going through divorces or having child problems because of work hours driven by an hours race that rewards inefficiency and 'face time' are unhappy."

"How do I access the documents?" Mark asked.

"Excellent!" Spunker nearly shouted and clapped Mark on the back. "A convert! Sit here." He motioned to a desk at the far end of the room where a desktop monitor was positioned.

"As you know," Spunker began, "everything is in the cloud. Accessible 24/7 by anyone in BFC. There are no personal filing systems since there are no personal hard drives. So we don't have any instances where documents are held on a lawyer's computer and then no one in the firm can get to them. We have even worked with our SaaS—software as a service—provider to develop a system whereby e-mails are automatically catalogued into the proper matter file folder. There are no situations where e-mails are sitting in a lawyer's personal e-mail accounts. All e-mails sit on a common folder accessible to all."

"That will certainly reduce the number of snarky e-mails," Mark said.

"Absolutely," replied Spunker. "There is no secrecy here, although each lawyer and staff member is given a private folder for personal e-mails. But back to what I was saying about the file systems. Take, for example, a client such as Terramound. We can click on Terramound and we will see all the files being worked on by the entire firm, subcategorized by specific matters. That way, support staff in the Philippines can access them and make changes for your review in the morning.

"And what you will be aware of when you have finished your avatar training is that we have a dummy portal set up for clients to see how our KM functions. It is set around a basic corporate acquisition and gives clients an idea of how we leverage our firm-approved documents as well as our research. You are free to use it at any time and in fact I encourage you to show it to clients as often as possible so that they can see our inner workings. They will be impressed. I can assure you of that. And a client that is impressed with efficiency is less likely to complain about our accounts and more likely to pay them in a timely fashion.

"In addition, we have created client-shared space within our servers, a separate, private cloud within the cloud, as it were."

Mark was intrigued by this point.

"We have a number of clients for whom we do a significant amount of work and who want a more hands-on approach to their files. So we give them, and the lawyers working on their matters, a separate cloud space in which to work. No one else has access to this space. All documents and all communication takes place in that space so the client knows exactly what is going on at all times. The space is easily accessible by the client and we've trained all lawyers and staff on its use."

Spunker tapped Mark on the shoulder and motioned him out of the room.

"The last things that you need to be aware of are our latest projects. And as a new member of BFC, I welcome your comments. We've been mandated by the executive to come up with ways to increase profits by leveraging KM in ways that do not involve lawyers." Mark looked confused by this concept. "Think about it," Barry continued. "We have all this data that we use only when we are retained on a file; otherwise it sits unused and unleveraged on our servers. So we are now in the process of packaging this data in a way that allows a wide variety of clients to access select areas of our KM on a subscription basis, effectively making KM a profit center without any additional hires and without using any manpower! Imagine a legal service provider that makes money while all of its lawyers are fast asleep, or on vacation, or working on someone else's file. Perhaps someday we can configure our KM systems so that we won't even need lawyers at all. Remember Warren Bennis's quote about factories of the future needing only a man and a dog?"

"I don't know that one," Mark replied.

Spunker smiled. "My modification is much better. The law firm of the future will need only a man and a dog. The man will feed the dog and the dog will keep the man away from the KM system." He laughed.

Mark kept his thoughts to himself. Surely the world would always need lawyers. But that's probably what the ice man thought before the creation of refrigerators.

"To drive that point home a little further," Barry continued, "we are investing in a new algorithmic program that will assist our research teams in India. Through quantitative legal prediction,[18] this program analyzes thousands of cases on any type of dispute and predicts the outcome of any dispute BFC is dealing with. That helps us save costs and increases the chances of a more favorable result for our clients. We can determine the likelihood of success with greater accuracy, and then negotiate accordingly. No team of human lawyers could ever do that!"

***

Mark walked back to his desk to grab his suit jacket. He had five minutes to meet Sylvester Bowen.

"How was your morning with Barry?" Stephen Boulder stuck his head over the top of the pod.

"He certainly loves his job."

"That he does. A little too much for my liking—I mean seriously, should you really like your job that much?"

"Don't you?" Mark shot back. "Isn't that why you're here?"

"Touché!"

Mark looked at his watch.

"Better hurry," Boulder said. "Bowen is a very precise guy and doesn't like to be kept waiting."

Mark rushed off to the lobby where the receptionist told him that Mr. Bowen would be fifteen minutes late.

"He's never on time," she confided to him.

---

[18] See Professor Daniel Katz's writings in this area at Computational Legal Studies, http://computationallegalstudies.com/.

CHAPTER 6
Lunch with Bowen

The restaurant menu contained a variety of pan-Asian delicacies. Mark wanted to choose something for lunch that wasn't messy, something that wouldn't make him look foolish in front of the boss; he opted for sushi.

They sat across from each other at an uncomfortably small table, small not only for both of them, but even for Bowen sitting alone. There was something supersized about the man that struck Mark immediately. Bowen's personality seemed to be larger than his six-foot-two frame. Since Mark was much shorter, they made for a very odd couple in the restaurant.

"Mark, I'm glad you're aboard," Sylvester Bowen said. "As Rachel may have told you, we don't hire students or junior lawyers; they are a pointless waste of money."

He said the words as if he was ordering a beer. Mark had never heard a senior lawyer make such a damning statement about students and junior lawyers in such a cavalier manner. But if Bowen saw the look of surprise on Mark's face, he didn't react to it.

"That makes you the most junior lawyer in our office."

Mark smiled, unsure if that was a compliment or not.

"Our preference," Bowen continued, "is to let other firms train you and pay you. Then, when we like what we see, we simply swoop in and pick through the litter." He stopped. "You look skeptical."

"Doesn't that put you at risk of holes in the firm?" Mark asked.

"Ah yes," Bowen said. He put his chopsticks gently down on his dish and leaned back in his chair. "The infamous 'hole theory.' I suppose that *if* we had decided to work in the way of an old-style firm, spending enormous amounts of money on young lawyers and students who give us no return on investment, and *if* we made them show us that they will spend their entire life in the office at the expense of everything they held dear before becoming a lawyer. . .." He stopped, letting the word "lawyer" hang in the air.

After a moment, Bowen added, "Then yes. You're right. We would be concerned about the scary and dangerous hole theory."

Mark wished that he hadn't raised the point. He had already forgotten the welcome screen on his computer: BFC performs similar legal services, but in a very different way. As much as he wanted to change and work in a different model of legal services, he still carried with him the baggage of eight years of prior practice.

"When Fong, Chandri, and I started this firm from the ashes of Garfield & Carmichael," Bowen continued, "we wanted to be different. We didn't buy into the old style of doing things. Some of that probably came from our backgrounds—all nonwhite kids from immigrant parents. Who were we kidding? We didn't have a hope in hell of making it in Big Law. Then we thought, Why did we even want to be in Big Law? Other than the money and prestige, what exactly was the point of it all? We decided that money and prestige were not enough for us—they were shallow reasons to practice law."

Bowen grabbed his chopsticks, picked a suitable piece of chicken, and dipped it into teriyaki sauce. "Our premise was simple: start from the basics," he said. "If there were no such thing as a law firm, how would the three of us create something that would provide legal services?"

"Pretty brash," Mark said.

"Agreed! But sometimes it helps to throw out the old models and start from scratch, especially when it appeared to us that those old models, while they may have been perfectly appropriate 1,000 years ago, when lawyers were created in hell, were no longer were valid."

Mark choked back a laugh.

Bowen continued. "But with advances in communications and technology, those models no longer made sense. The concept of law as a calling, rather than a business, should have gone out in the last century, but there are still those who cling to that quaint notion; it colors everything that they do, from how they structure the firm, to how they charge, to how they operate. If you take that notion away, then you have the freedom to view law for what it really is—a service business—period, full stop."

"But what's wrong with the idea of law as a calling?" Mark added.

"Nothing—as long as lawyers don't consider themselves to be above everyone else by virtue of 'being called.' A sense of entitlement and arrogance is an unfortunate legacy of law. But if you think about the practice of law as simply a business that provides services, that mindset changes. No businessperson would dare suggest that he was 'called' to operate an Internet company, for example."

Mark was warming to Sylvester Bowen. The man was passionate, not about some arcane aspect of law, but how law should be practiced. It was a refreshing change from the discussions at his old firm where case law, hours, and money were the mainstays of conversation.

"Fong had an MBA and Chandri had an IT background. As for me," Bowen said, raising a cup of tea, "I've just got flaky ideas on how law is supposed to be practiced."

Mark nearly choked on the California roll he was chewing.

"Everything okay?" Bowen asked.

Mark nodded and reached for his tea. "The wasabi," he gasped, pointing to the green blob on his dish. "It's really strong here. Caught me off guard."

"Be careful," Bowen cautioned. He drank some tea before adding, "I hope that you didn't receive a dream from God, Allah, Buddha, or whatever you believe in, to go to law school—did you?"

"No," Mark replied. In a sheepish tone he added, "I had the grades and, being unsure of what else to do with a masters in political science, I went to law school. I hardly felt called. And I never felt a need to 'right' injustice. I just wanted to do some interesting things."

"Then you've come to the right place." Bowen seemed pleased with the response. "We do interesting things, but just as importantly, we properly allocate resources to do them."

He took another sip of tea.

"Let me give you the five-minute history of BFC since it is very unlikely that you have had the time to read much of our bible. It's much more detailed there and has some nice photos."

Bowen cleared his throat and composed himself. He clearly had a set speech that he gave on this topic.

"Chandri saw the rise of legal process outsourcers in his native India years ago and immediately made the connection that a law firm could benefit by the thoughtful outsourcing of routine and repetitive tasks. Fong, God rest his soul, was really keen on knowledge management. You've met Barry Spunker already and I'm sure he has told you everything that you could ever want to know about KM and more."

"He's definitely passionate," Mark said.

"I'm just the strategy guy," Bowen continued. "The guy who pulls it all together. I haven't practiced in years. In fact I doubt that anyone would even let me near a file now." He laughed before sipping more tea.

"But I digress. As I alluded to earlier, Fong, Chandri, and I were once like you, young lawyers in the land of Big Law trying to make sense of it all. But we found that we really couldn't. A lot of what we did, and saw being done in firms, didn't make sense to us and that added to our general malaise. Unhappy lawyers don't do good work. Unhappy lawyers aren't passionate about their work. Unhappy lawyers reflect poorly on the firm and clients *do* notice. While I couldn't always be in control of what I was doing with my professional life, I needed to know that there was some logic and common sense in how things operated. That was important to me. I wasn't a drone that mindlessly followed the same old processes, did things the same way without thought. I refused to accept that there was only one way to do things or that change was bad. Do you understand?"

Mark nodded as he munched on a salmon roll.

"Those aren't the kinds of lawyers that we want at BFC. And that's why we push all of you to keep thinking up new ways to do things—better, faster, cheaper. It's not a coincidence that the acronym for better, faster, cheaper is BFC."

Bowen plucked a small piece of chicken from his bowl and quickly ate it.

"That's why," he continued, "our bonus structure has nothing to do with hours and everything to do with allowing us to provide better client service, whether it's through efficiency, redesignation of tasks, or better KM. Working hard for the sake of working hard doesn't cut it at BFC. Anyone can work hard."

Bowen waved his chopsticks in the air in a dismissive manner.

"As clichéd as it sounds, we reward those who work smarter, and not everyone can do that. If we see someone continuously working late or working on weekends, that's a problem; either with the lawyer or it signals that we need to add capacity."

He stopped, inviting Mark to comment.

"That's what attracted me to BFC in the first place: the ability to keep thinking, instead of being a grunt."

A waiter came to ask if everything was all right at the table. Bowen confirmed that everything was "excellent."

When the waiter had left, Bowen asked Mark, "Tell me, what was important to keeping your career alive at the other firm?"

"Face time. Always being seen to be working nights, weekends."

"Perfect—so what does that teach you?" Bowen scowled.

"To not be so good at your job that you can have a life."

"Let me give you a much better answer," Bowen said. "It teaches you to be inefficient and creates a culture of waste. Time is no longer a precious commodity. It is there to be squandered, because the more time you squander, the more money you make. Whereas the business model of every other successful business on the planet is based upon saving time and money in the processes that create a product, lawyers take the opposite approach.

"For centuries, lawyers were better educated and could hold the mystique of law over others because no one else could understand it. But times change. All sorts of legal information is disseminated for free and people are better able to understand it. There are more in-house lawyers than ever before; they understand the law and how law firms operate. The mystique is wearing thin. And when the mystique wears off, clients are less willing to pay extra for it. Nothing made me crazier than to be doing a function at my old firm that I knew was worth nowhere near what I was going to charge the client. The task was not something that required my expertise as a lawyer, but I needed the hours to preserve my job and the firm was unwilling to invest in a business model that would push this task to someone who was much more cost effective."

"I know exactly how you feel," Mark interjected.

"So," Bowen continued, "it made sense to me and the others that we needed a different structure at BFC because it is the structure of the firm, not just the tone at the top, that shapes how people work; structure changed the drivers, which changed the behaviors.

"Our corporate model," Bowen continued, "gives us a huge advantage because it causes us to think as a company, not individually. The partnership model has no room for any element of custodianship, teamwork, or collaboration. At BFC we have shifted away from the concepts of ownership and rights, and toward custodianship, stewardship, responsibility, and accountability.[19] Only a corporate structure can actually achieve this, as human nature, left to its own devices, will often default to greed and self-interest. A partner on the cusp of retirement clearly has different interests from those of a new partner, and the interests of a litigation partner will be at odds with those in, say, real estate, particularly in a recession, when litigation work is rampant but real estate work no longer exists.

"But also from the standpoint of making good decisions, a partnership makes little sense; having large numbers of partners vote on firm decisions is not only inefficient, it is not in the best interests of the firm as a whole. It's akin to herding cats. Democracy may be good for a country but it plays hell with business entities. That's why we have an independent board of directors at BFC. The board forces decisions to be made for the good of BFC as a whole, independent of the personal agendas of individual lawyers within the firm. Directors do not fear retribution from other lawyers within BFC for the decisions they make because they are independent of the firm. In fact, they are all general counsel of major companies.

"All of this leads to my ultimate goal. We must leave BFC in better shape than when we found it. Or to put it another way,

---

[19] STEPHEN MAYSON, MAKING SENSE OF LAW FIRMS 522.

we do not own BFC; we are merely borrowing it from the next generation of lawyers and staff."

Mark was stunned. Had Bowen really said that he was merely borrowing BFC from future generations? He had never heard any lawyer, let alone a name partner, ever speak in such a way. Bowen was right. In a traditional law office, no one cared about the firm once they had left, so there was no incentive to invest in the firm if a partner was not going to reap immediate benefits.

"Do you know why the partnership model is doomed to failure?" Bowen said, pointing his chopsticks at Mark.

Mark began to answer but was cut off.

"The collective action dilemma."[20]

"I don't know what that is," Mark replied.

"The collective action dilemma is where you have a group of people all acting in a perfectly rational way for their own interests in the short term."

"Okay," Mark replied, not at all sure why that was a problem.

"Take a law firm, for instance. Everyone just goes out and does their own thing in their own self-interest, year after year. Getting clients where they can, billing time, collecting fees, and taking out profits at the end of the year."

Mark nodded again, still not seeing any difficulty.

"And they believe if they do that, the firm will be in good shape; they believe that their actions when all put together will keep the firm afloat in perpetuity. However, in terms of long-term strategy, this is a completely irrational way to act. The short-term goals of individual lawyers do not automatically lead to the long-term viability of the firm because individual lawyers do not care what happens to the firm after they leave. So there is a disincentive for lawyers to act in a way that assures the long-term interest of the firm, because acting in the long-term interests of the firm

---

[20] *See* MANCUR OLSON, THE LOGIC OF COLLECTIVE ACTION.

will reduce the amount of money that each lawyer makes in the short term.

"When firms were small—say, three to five lawyers—the actions of that small group of lawyers would be aligned with the long-term interests of the firm since the long-term interests of a small firm was a great benefit to those lawyers; it gave them a living. But in an era of large firms employing hundreds of lawyers, that is no longer the case."

Mark nodded his head in agreement.

"And success further compounds the problem," Bowen continued. "When a firm is successful using the partnership model, there is vindication of that model. And each successful year perpetuates a sense that this is the correct model and that feeds itself in a closed loop. The motto 'we've always done this in the past, and it worked' reinforces the belief that it will continue to work in the future; previous success reinforces bad models. George Soros would call this a double feedback, reflexive connection. This gives law firms a distorted sense of reality, or what passes for reality, in how they should do business, how they should structure the business, and what clients actually want, simply because they have created that reality for themselves.[21]

"With our competitors, the assets of the firm are the individual partners, which leads to their being paid insanely huge amounts of money, sometimes with little payback. But partners are mobile. There is little to keep them in the firm and they can simply jump from firm to firm, to whoever gives them the most money. That money in turn, affects the fees to be paid by the clients. So, greed, rather than proper business practice, is driving pricing to clients."

---

[21] *See* Timothy Garton Ash, *Look out for Another Financial Avalanche,* GLOBE & MAIL, June 24, 2010, http://www.theglobeandmail.com/news/opinions/look-out-for-another-financial-avalanche/article1615224/ ("Realities create expectations, but expectations also create realities, and so on.").

Bowen stabbed at another piece of chicken, then grasped it with his chopsticks. Holding the chicken in the air, he continued.

"How secure is it for a firm to take in a partner who has no loyalty to the firm—one who is only loyal to herself? Who could, at a moment's notice, leave with a number of associates and staff, thereby putting a hole in a firm's practice group?"

"Not very," Mark said.

"This is another reason why the partnership model is a flawed and extremely unstable form of business model. It creates a balkanized culture whereby departments fight over the pieces of the pie that they brought to the table, then split off to join another firm when they feel they are not making enough money."

He put the piece of chicken into his mouth.

"I didn't want to create a firm that would be blown apart by the greed of a new group of partners, twenty or thirty years from now," he said. "That's what happened at Garfield & Carmichael. But if you turn the system on its head as we have done at BFC, and make individual lawyers less important than the firm as a whole, then individual lawyers have far less power and far less leverage for stupid salaries. It forces a team approach because in order to succeed we all have to work together in preserving and enhancing our KM and our systems. We all have to work together to create efficiencies that will in turn generate greater profit that can then be shared among all.

"It is only when we acknowledge that the firm and its systems are more important than any specific lawyer that true teamwork results, and the selfish, self-centered approach to practicing law will end. Does it end politics within the firm? Probably not. But since there is no longer any power associated with client ownership, it does reduce the toxicity. It's not perfect, but it's a better system than that of our competitors."

Bowen picked through his food. He was talking through most of the lunch and there was still plenty for him to finish. But it seemed to Mark that Bowen was not comfortable with silence. He seemed to need to fill it at all costs. Before long he was speaking again.

"We also took away the petty annoyances."

"Like timekeeping," Mark said.

"Bingo. I always felt that keeping track of time was itself, a waste of time. It's far from accurate and drives negative behavior. It makes good people do bad things. Instead of offering an incentive to lawyers to get their work done as efficiently as possible so that they can save the client money and allow them to leave the office, timekeeping dehumanizes a lawyer. His worth is measured solely by the number of hours he can record each month."

He pointed a chopstick at Mark. "How many good, effective lawyers at your old firm had consistently low hours?"

"None," Mark said. "They wouldn't last very long if their hours were low."

"Exactly. Hours were the sole measure of productivity, not client satisfaction, not effective work, not contribution to KM, and certainly not any contribution to professional development; all the things that would continue to add value to the firm for years were ignored. But much more insidious is the fact that you get what you measure. If you measure hours you will get hours, and if a lawyer creates a benefit that cannot be measured in billable hours, then that effort is seen to be worthless.

"Freedom from keeping track of hours at BFC gives us the opportunity to readjust our thinking: to find, and place value on, other activities. It creates a cultural shift among our team. We work for the common good of the firm. If billable hours are no longer important, competition among lawyers for those hours breaks down. Lawyers become more willing to help other lawyers, as such work is not a drain on your hours' quota. And a client does not have to pay an additional fee when a senior lawyer helps out with a more junior project. Lawyers at BFC no longer ask as their first question, 'What's the client matter number?' It's, 'How can I help?'

"Back when I did legal work, I once had a first-year lawyer defend his firm's outrageously high bill for a cookie-cutter deal on the basis that he had spent a lot of time on the file. In his mind, his time, no matter inefficiently managed, was valuable, even if it was his inexperience alone that caused him to spend too much time on a file. He completely missed the fact that my client—who was required to pay the account—did not see any value in his work and was therefore was unwilling to pay for it. Now it might be said that all juniors should do this because it is for the responsible senior partner to recognize that the work did not justify the fee and adjust it—but that rarely happens.

"That's why," he continued, "we have a different matrix when assessing BFC lawyers; it's result-oriented. Did the lawyer achieve her personal goals, which, in turn, are aligned to the firm's goals? Those goals are broken down in different categories such as professional development, client development, management administration, and so on. Lawyers are rewarded for what they have done—not how much time they have spent on any category."

"That was another reason why I found BFC attractive," Mark said. "I never truly understood how my old firm determined my pay or that of others."

"People will do what we pay them to do," Bowen replied. "At most firms, people are paid to bill hours; as a result, the firm gets more hours—but do the clients get quality results? We had to take a completely different approach because we do not bill by the hour. We identified behaviors we wanted at BFC. Once those were identified we prepared a compensation model that would drive those types of behavior, while also ensuring that the model was transparent and consistent throughout BFC and aligned with our overall business strategy. The role of our compensation model is not to pay our team, it's to assist in achieving our short and long-term strategy by driving the right culture, the right results, and the right performance. We spent a great deal of effort fine-tuning the model and then revisiting it when we saw that we were unintentionally incenting negative behavior. So we always ask ourselves if our compensation philosophy supports BFC's strategy and question if our performance measures motivate our team to get the desired result. If we do our job right, we end up with a rational and defensible policy that all staff and lawyers not only understand, but also feel is fair and balanced.

"How does the share purchase plan come into play?" Mark asked.

"Lawyers are invited to purchase shares in BFC and are designated with a vice president title, instead of being called a partner. As for salary, everyone at the same pay grade—there are several grades—receives the same base salary and they all have the chance to receive bonuses, based on achievement of BFC's overall corporate goals, achievement of their group's goal, and achievement of their personal goals. It's a transparent process to reduce conflict over remuneration and takes out the subjective element that often plagues firm remuneration. In this way we cultivate lawyers who care about the firm's goals, because at BFC, hitting personal goals is only one part of the bonus formula. This approach not only encourages buy-in to the overall strategic goals of the firm, it also creates a strong sense of the team and encourages everyone to take ownership in the firm's results and share in the firm's success."

Bowen stopped for another sip of his tea.

"Now," Bowen lowered his voice and leaned across the table. "Let me throw something else out at you that may seem somewhat radical."

Mark wasn't sure how much more radical a law firm could get, but he was open to more change. He was really starting to like the outlook of the firm.

"Another reason why I don't like time sheets is because they are shackles around the ankles of lawyers."

Mark smiled. "I thought I was the only one who thought of time sheets in that way."

"You can dress up the concept of time sheets as a way to make money," Bowen said. "And as a way to place some value on the work product. But what it ultimately does is police lawyers—to ensure that they are working. Low hours means that the lawyer is clearly goofing off. Right?"

Mark nodded.

"Wrong! If you liberate lawyers from accounting for every second of their existence, you foster trust among your team. I don't need to know what you're doing every minute of the day. I just need to know the clients are happy, the work is getting done, and we're making money. Period. How the lawyer chooses to achieve those goals is not important to me—unless of course she is doing something illegal or unprofessional.

"And with the virtual way in which BFC operates, trust and autonomy are paramount. We trust our people to do their jobs in the best way they see fit. We don't need to watch them do it. If the job isn't done, the clients will complain or another member of the team will complain that something is missing. That is the check and balance. Risky, some might say."

Mark shrugged his shoulders.

"My view is that it is more risky to not trust your team members and thereby destroy their enthusiasm. People who aren't trusted aren't happy, and unhappy workers are less productive. Trust tells the team members that they are important and valued. Have we been taken advantage of? Of course, but not often. That is the risk we accept, and those persons are no longer with us.

"Removing the shackles also gives lawyers the freedom to do things that they would never do if they had to account for their time. Client visits are a huge part of our vision here. Lawyers who are not busy with work take time to visit clients and see how they can be helpful to those clients without worrying about accounting for their time. In fact, most of our new work comes from existing clients. Surprise, surprise," Bowen said, bobbing his head to add to the sarcasm. "And that is because BFC lawyers go out to client offices, learn about their business, and make helpful suggestions. The more time we invest in getting to know our clients and their businesses, the better able we are to identify risks that are around the bend for them.

"But it's also the little things that make a big difference in how clients perceive us. And, as I'm sure Rachel told you, one of those things is disbursements."

Bowen paused and shook his head as if he was remembering a bad experience. "I was often embarrassed to send a bill to a client for $30,000 and then tack on $25 for fax charges and $5 for postage. It's like a courier company charging for gas, tire wear, and oil changes in addition to the courier charges. Surely these are administrative costs that a firm should absorb and factor into their fee? So you will notice that we do not charge for disbursements, except for government charges such as registration fees, filing fees, and the like. It's a little thing, but it sends a big message to clients: BFC doesn't nickel and dime you. We care about you and we care enough about our business model to make sure that the fee that you are charged covers all our costs."

"You won't get any complaints from me about that," Mark said.

Bowen continued. "There is a small bagel shop around the corner from where David and I live. Montreal-style bagels, you know the ones? A hint of honey glazing to give the bagel just a little extra zip?"

"Yes, I love those, actually," Mark said. "You'll have to give me the name."

"I will," Bowen responded. "But my point has got nothing to do with bagels. If I come into the shop to buy my poppy-seed bagel and coffee, and I don't have enough money, do they ask for the bagel back? No! They say, 'Don't worry about being a bit short. Catch us next time.' And when I come in with my grandniece, they give her a free bagel."

"Nice," Mark replied.

"Exactly, nice. Do I go back and buy my bagels from that guy, or do I go somewhere else?"

"You go back," Mark answered.

"Right," Bowen said. "Now, when I go to the bank and I have a problem, my account manager immediately fixes it. Does she waive fees for me? Yes! Now, would I go to another bank?"

Mark shook his head.

"Exactly. I saw all these things and I realized that as lawyers we did not treat our clients in the same manner. We carefully – and in many cases, carelessly – record our time to ensure that we *properly* bill clients for our work. It rarely occurs to us to say, 'Don't worry about it,' because then *we* have to worry about making up time spent helping a client *gratis*.

"Let me leave you with one more point. I was reading the *New York Times Magazine* one Sunday, and in the back was an advertisement for an investment advisor, the name of which completely escapes me now, but the ad was a simple one. It said very elegantly: *The lower the costs, the more you keep.* Exceptionally obvious. But it needed to be said. If the advisor lowers her management costs, the client makes more money. So, I thought, if a lawyer lowers his costs, he makes more money. Yet the philosophy of law firms at that time, and still today, is 'The higher the hourly rate, the more money we make.'"

Mark picked up the tea pot and poured more tea into Bowen's cup.

"Cost control," Bowen continued, "is thought of only in terms of cutting lawyers and staff when there is a downturn in the economy. There is no method to the madness. And since there is no method, employee morale plummets, which affects work product and, eventually, clients. When you cut a swath out of your team, it sends a message that you don't know what you're doing—you have no idea how to properly control your costs because if you did, you wouldn't be firing anyone.

"Our cost control allows us to weather financial storms much better and keep our personnel intact—which increases staff morale.

"BFSigma was instrumental in allowing us to send routine and repetitive work and even our legal research to our LPO, so that we significantly reduced our overhead and hired lawyers here only to do high-level legal work and perform management/client functions. In fact, you will find that you are more like a legal consultant here than a lawyer. You'll be spending some time in India soon and you'll meet Chandri when you are there; he spends most of the year in India.

"Our LPO is not only a way to reduce our overhead, it's also another profit center for BFC, directly searching out routine work from clients with sophisticated legal departments that just need extra bodies to do work such as due diligence. In that case, they don't have to use BFC proper. They deal directly with the LPO, while having the comfort that it's a BFC operation, but without full BFC fees; some call it BFC Lite."

Mark was amazed that BFC was unbundling its legal services in this way. It had never occurred to his old firm to invest in a low-cost legal services provider as a way to retain clients.

Mark continued to eat his salmon roll while Bowen repeated his theory in various contexts. Mark made sure to make regular eye contact and murmur the occasional "uh-huh" to signify that he was still listening.

Maybe, Mark thought, his unhappiness at his old firm was structural, and not an indictment of the practice of law itself. Perhaps it was the distorted way in which law firms operated that had turned him against a profession that he was so eager to enter into eight years ago - after nearly being bankrupted by exorbitant tuition fees.

CHAPTER 7
Coach Kwan

Nancy Kwan arrived early at BFC to catch a session with the new yoga instructor. She felt that she needed some extra stress release before meeting with Mark Reynolds to run through BFC's value-based billing basics. He wasn't the first lawyer that she had been assigned to mentor, but newbies were always a challenge.

As much as she wanted to keep a clear mind through the yoga class, she couldn't help thinking back to her prior discussions with Mark about BFSigma. As BFSigma training was a full program run by much more qualified personnel than herself, her goal was simply to give a basic explanation to Mark so that he could understand the value of the program and what it involved.

The discussion had started without much problem. BFSigma was a proprietary lean sigma program that was designed specifically for BFC. The principles behind BFSigma were the same as those of lean sigma; which, in its simplest form, is a way to improve all processes at BFC. How can BFC reduce waste? How can BFC continue to improve? And how can BFC learn to look at value in the same way that a client does?

Mark seemed to like the overarching principles associated with BFSigma, but Nancy could see his eyes glaze over when she provided more detail about the frameworks that are used for

BFSigma: the creation of a project charter, DMAIC,[22] SIPOC,[23] and VoC,[24] among others.

BFSigma's real value, in Nancy's mind, was not to make every lawyer an expert in it—an outcome that was both impossible and unnecessary, as BFC kept five experts on staff, the so-called Black Belt BFSigmas—but rather to make sure it ingrained within all lawyers and staff a culture of continuous improvement. It reminded everyone that the job of looking for efficiencies and improvement was never-ending. And that job was just as important as the legal work undertaken by BFC.

So, as Mark quickly lost attention and focus, she decided to cut the matter short and simply ensure that he set up a training session with one of the black belts. "It's a rigorous way of thinking that forces you to methodically move through a process without jumping to a conclusion," was how she left it with him.

Their discussion about legal project management fared better, as it was much easier to understand. At its core, she explained to him, was the need to increase predictability so that a file could be properly priced. For every file, BFC needed to get a good handle on the main elements: resources, risk, timing, and scope.

If BFC lawyers did a proper job of settling the scope of the project with a client, the rest should flow into place. Proper scope allowed lawyers to not only allocate personnel (inside BFC as well as outsourced staff) but also assess any potential risks. Proper scope also allowed lawyers to identify any constraints on their

---

[22] DMAIC is an acronym for Define (the concern or problem), Measure (the performance of the existing process), Analyze (those opportunities that exist to reduce waste), Improve (the process through finding and using new processes), and Control (the new process so that the improvements will not disappear).

[23] Suppliers, Inputs, Process Steps, Outputs, and Clients.

[24] Voice of the Customer.

ability to perform the task and to assess the value that could be given to the client.

"Sounds pretty sensible and basic," Mark had said. "But don't we do this all the time in our heads at old-style firms?"

"Yes," Nancy had replied. "And that's the problem. We did it in our heads, which meant that we did it quickly, without methodology, skipping steps as we went through it, perhaps missing risks. And to be fair, when lawyers were billing by the hour, legal project management didn't have much application other than as a rough guide to estimate costs. But because it was just an estimate and not binding upon the firm, there was no point spending time mapping out what actually happens on a file, with dates, benchmarks, and personnel responsibilities."

Mark agreed that there was indeed little point in old-style firms spending any time on a process that made no difference to how much the client was going to pay. "And they would then have to bill their time for walking through the process," he said.

"But," Nancy continued, "when you have a value-based billing system, as we do at BFC, legal process management is critical not only to setting a fair fee, but to ensuring that BFC is a profitable entity. If we get it wrong on the project management piece, then we're going to waste our staff and lose money. And I do not want to have that kind of a conversation with the executive team—to explain how we didn't methodically go through exactly what the client was looking for in assessing the timelines and risks."

"Ouch," Mark said. "I never want to have that conversation either."

"The more uncertain we are about things," Nancy said, "the greater the risk that we price the file incorrectly. On the other hand, a legal project management system forces BFC and the client to have a dialogue on exactly what work is to be done, which eliminates any 'I thought you were, or were not, going to do that' comments afterwards. It also helps explain additional costs to the client when the client makes a change in the work requested."

She had brought with her a sample project management plan for a complex financing that she headed up last year. "I had a client tell me something a few years ago that has stuck with me ever since. It puts the importance of a legal project management system into more context. The client said, 'I am not going to be a passive consumer of someone else's legal services.' In other words, she wanted legal services that were tailored to her and the only sure-fire way to get that result is through a legal process management system."

Nancy showed Mark a Gantt chart setting out the scheduled timing of a transaction across actual calendar dates and a spreadsheet listing deliverables and responsibilities. There was enough detail to show the client who was to do what part of the transaction and when and how it was to be done: a complete road map to the deal.

"Please tell me that there's an app for this!" Mark said. "Or that we have plans for all the files that we typically do here."

"Of course we do!" she answered. "Why do you think we keep Barry Spunker around? He's got our KM system down to such a degree that we can access the project plans for every single file ever opened by the firm, as well as the pricing for those projects, together with the final reporting notes to understand if there were factors that were not taken into consideration for pricing, or that arose unexpectedly. He also has the team leader's comments on price and client satisfaction. We can group these plans and information according to geography, client, year and project type. The ability to access that kind of data quickly and effortlessly is invaluable when it comes to pricing out new work and building the most efficient and appropriate team."

She reached out to pat him on the shoulder. "When we say we don't reinvent the wheel here, we really mean it. Legal project management is critical to our success. Without it there is no standard practice across any large departments or across any offices. How many times did you sit down with your colleagues at your old firm and discuss how each of you completed a transaction?"

"Never."

"Right, because you all know how to close a transaction. But each of you takes different steps to achieve that result; some good, some bad. Legal process management creates firm unity as it forces us to all read from the same playbook and allows us to all collaborate on making the system better. It generates discussion among teams about best practices."

"But we already have checklists for our deals," Mark said.

"It's more than a checklist, Mark. It sets out the time needed to do certain items and details exactly who will deliver what and in what time frame so that proper sequencing can be sorted out. It also forces the parties to create a communication strategy between lawyers and clients for those times when a client states that all communication must go through a single source. With a Gantt chart you can point out that there are certain moments during the timeline that the client may wish to dispense with such a rigid rule. Most importantly, legal process management forces a post project review to not only assess client satisfaction but how to improve next time."

"And figure out what things to send to Barry and his KM team," Mark added.

"Well done," she replied.

"And I suppose that also helps explain pricing to the client as well?"

"Now you're catching on, Mark." She was happy to see that he was finally grasping how a variety of things were connecting.

"Our pricing is not simply pulling numbers out of the air, and our clients should never see it as that. With the data we have in place, we can say, for example, to client ABC Corp, 'We have done ten deals just like this in that part of the country and the pricing for those deals were X and so that is what we will charge you.' Put that conversation together with a Gantt chart and a responsibility spreadsheet, and confidence in our ability to do the task skyrockets. We can look at who worked on that deal, what portions were home-sourced, and what parts were sent to India, and we can reassemble the team quickly. We can show the client the team that we're using and why we're using them—namely that they've worked on similar deals that have come in at the budgeted amount."

Nancy pulled her laptop from her briefcase and motioned Mark to come beside her. When the computer had fully loaded she clicked a link entitled Expertise.

"Don't forget this puppy," she said. "Which, by the way, you will be inserted into once you have given me your legal expertise list." She gave him a stern look. "By tomorrow, okay?"

Mark nodded.

"In this," she continued, pointing to the folder, "you can instantly find out the appropriate expertise within the firm should you ever need it. Every lawyer and her expertise is listed here. Then cross-reference that with the exact deals that the lawyer has worked on in the database. What is the BFC mantra?"

"BFC performs legal services that differ from those of our rivals; or similar legal services, but in a very different way."

"Good," she replied. Then added, "Look, Mark, I'm sorry if this feels like grade school, with me asking you to repeat mantras, but it really is the best way to stretch your brain so that it doesn't shrink back into the old habits that you formed at your old firm."

"I hear you. It's a big change for me. Bigger than I expected, actually." He looked down at the project management plans that Nancy had given him and then looked up again at her.

"I suppose there's another way that we can use these plans and all the data."

"Go on," she said. "I'm listening."

"You said that we use the data to show clients that we've done several similar deals in order to validate our pricing of their deal."

She nodded.

"I suppose with a client that does a high volume of work—like a bank, or a company that does a number of acquisitions regularly each year, or trademark and patent work—we'll have the data on these matters."

"Correct."

"So, each year, we can demonstrate value-added by pointing out to the client how we have improved our processes and timing—year over year." He smiled and added excitedly, "And we can also show how, year over year, our increased efficiencies have resulted in not only lower costs to the client, but also faster results."

"Well done!"

But Mark wasn't finished. "We could even bundle up a report to the general counsel each year showing the improvement year over year, one that she would be able to turn around and send to her board, or senior management, to make her look good. A sort of annual report to the client."

"Perfect! We make general counsel look good to her company and that makes BFC look fantastic to her." She was impressed. "Now I do have a question for you and I want you to be completely honest."

"Sure, what's that?"

"Who are you, and what have you done with Mark Reynolds?"

***

After her yoga class, Nancy met Mark at his desk.

She started off in a gentle voice. "The past week we've gone through an awful lot that is completely new to you. All of it funnels down to our main objective, which is to undertake value-based billing."

"Sure, alternative billing is BFC's special sauce," Mark replied, remembering Barry Spunker's comment with respect to KM.

"Not alternative billing," Nancy said. "Value-based billing. Alternative billing can be anything, and that *anything* doesn't require a value-based approach. Value-based billing says it all in a succinct way. Our charges are based on value. So, use that term always, especially when meeting new and potential clients."

"Will do," Mark said.

"Okay," Nancy said. "Test time. You've read through our materials by now, so tell me what value-based billing methods we typically use at BFC."

"Fixed fee," Mark replied feeling confident that today was going to be easier than the previous ones. He was very interested in the different ways that lawyers could charge for value rather than based on hours, so he had been able to absorb the BFC materials on this topic fairly easily.

"Example?" Nancy asked.

"This can be used in any legal matter provided that the appropriate legal project management plan has been prepared. But it is most often used for transactional matters where there is little risk of unknown elements coming into play."

"What about litigation?" She had to stop herself from sounding too much like a Marine Corps drill instructor.

"If you had asked me that at my old firm I would have said no."

"And now?"

"Now I say, why not?" Mark's voice was confident. "Knowing that most litigation settles, we can skinny the file, reduce wasted effort, and eliminate procedures that won't enhance settlement. We can set a fee for the entire matter or do it piecemeal for each step of the way; so much money for pleadings, so much per motion, so much for discoveries."

"The key?"

"Again, the key is legal project management as well as BFSigma."

"Not bad," she said. "But that was an easy one. What else have you got?"

Mark chuckled. "I've got lots. How about monthly fees?"

"That sounds interesting. What is it?" Nancy asked, trying to act like she had never heard of the concept.

"We can charge a monthly fee for any and all work done in the month, typically used for routine compliance-type matters that recur. And if you pay us in advance on the first of the month, I can swing you an even better deal because I like predictable cash-flow with no payment waiting time."

"Another?"

"If we have pools of work, say in trademarks or repetitive litigation, we can set fees based on the predictability of the work; and we can create performance-related fees with a fee-at-risk component that allows us to get a bonus, or penalty, depending upon if we hit, or miss, milestones."

"Excellent. So that's it, right?"

"Absolutely not! We can make up any variation of these or come up with new ones. There is no limit."

"Benefits to clients?"

"Predictability of fees, which facilitates budgeting."

"And?"

"It eliminates any need to police accounts as the fee is already agreed upon and the disbursements are few and far between."

Nancy gave Mark a congratulatory slap on the back.

"Excellent. As a reward, we're bidding on a new RFP from Kowtor Industries and you're going to be the one writing up the response—if we're short-listed, you'll be on the client team."

PART III

CHAPTER 8
Bowen's Swan Song

Bowen was the first to notice the newcomer.

"Kimberly," he called out as she wheeled herself onto the rooftop deck of the BFC building.

"Welcome to BFC. Let me get you a drink." He waved to the barman.

"This is a nice idea, dinner under the stars on a roof-top deck," she said. "And please, call me Kim."

"Thank you. We always have a directors' dinner the night before our board meeting. It allows the directors to get to know each other and our senior management team in a more relaxed atmosphere. It's hard to form good relationships in just six meetings a year. This event gives us extra time to foster good ideas and, on an informal basis, sort out some questions that may come up in the board package."

"I must admit that I didn't know what to expect when I joined your board," Kim said. "BFC has a reputation for being very different from its competitors, but I did receive some very good reports from former directors of your board. And I did read your article in the BFC bible about corporate governance. Interesting ideas."

"That's kind of you. But the piece wasn't very good."

Bowen looked across the room as the barman handed Kim her drink. Bowen motioned for her to accompany him across the deck.

"It seems that everyone is here now. Our board is relatively small—just nine directors, including an independent chair; all of them are general counsel from companies in the area, but a few from out of town. We try to ensure that the board receives perspectives from a wide range of industries. You may know some of them already."

"Actually I only know them by reputation," Kim said. "Not personally."

Bowen continued on. "We're delighted to have your skill set on the board. As you know, everyone on the board is a lawyer—a rather stupid rule put in place by the law society but one that, I'm sure, over time will eventually disappear."

He waved his hand irreverently in the air as if he were shooing away a bothersome insect. "Along with the ban on third-party investment; we're always getting inquiries from investors who want to become shareholders in BFC."

"Dare to dream."

"Ah." Bowen leaned his head back to give an exaggerated look into the sky. "But in the meantime, we continue to operate like a real business, because we believe that operating as a business entity whose interests are paramount to those within the organization is the best way for law firms to be run. Or, let me put it another way. The existing models of firm operations do not represent reality; they are merely constructions of a reality preferred by those in power at law firms."[25]

"Now you're getting a little too deep for me," Kim said.

"Sorry, it was an excellent concept that I read somewhere and I always wanted to spring it on someone," Bowen replied. "I really just dabble, put together pieces and hope that things work out. What I think it means is that the way firms operate today is not the only way to operate them. They operate in that fashion because that form of operation creates a benefit for those who manage the firms. But just because we operate one way today,

---

[25] See Roger Martin, The Opposable Mind 115.

doesn't mean that we'll operate that way in the future. Better models will always arise and as long as we have created a culture in which we are constantly striving for change, a culture in which change is embraced, not feared, we will always gain first-mover advantage over our competitors."

"You don't sound like a law firm at all."

"No slave to precedents and the past here."

"BFC's value-based billing struck me as very interesting," Kim said. "Something I would like to explore with the firms we use. It's unfortunate that I can't use BFC for my work until I leave the board."

"Absolutely," Bowen replied. "That's a conflict that we would not permit. And you would not be the first to send us work after finishing on our board. We've had a number of clients come to us from former board members. After being immersed in the workings of our firm, they gain confidence in our capabilities and generally switch their work to us."

"So this is a marketing ploy as well?"

He smiled. "There is no reality, remember? Just perceptions. But yes, if we happen to derive some benefit from having a board composed solely of general counsel, then I'm happy to accept it. But it's a two-way street; we also gain a greater appreciation for what clients value most."

"Ah, we're a captive focus group."

"Far better than a focus group or client survey; and with greater pay!" Bowen was quick to point out.

"Yes, I was surprised that the board remuneration was consistent with industry standards." Kim had served on a number of boards in the past and was genuinely surprised at the generous director fees paid by BFC.

"I'm surprised that you're surprised," Bowen responded. "After all, it would be presumptuous of us to expect you to work and provide your insights for free. We don't consider this board to be some silly blue ribbon advisory panel, where we slap each other on the backs over martinis twice a year. It's very real and the directors really work, so they should be paid accordingly."

"Oh, I'm not disputing that," Kim exclaimed. "The board materials were very substantial."

"It's also why we instituted the director share purchase requirement, so that each of you have skin in the game; a real stake in BFC."

"It certainly makes me pay attention to what's happening on a board," Kim replied. "And to not be shy about giving my opinion."

"That's what we're looking for; it's one of our competitive advantages."

"It must make for an interesting dynamic and culture, no?" she asked. "I assume that the lawyers in BFC are less likely to rebel against directors who may be potential clients in the future."

"Absolutely correct. It's difficult to complain if directions are coming from potential clients, even if you don't like what's being said. We listen to our clients here, and if changes need to be made—they are."

Kim nodded, then added, "I'm with you 100 percent in connection with a corporate structure and management style. But I do have some concern over the LPO arrangement—BFC Lite—and home-sourcing. Are we really able to control quality, and maintain confidentiality and privacy? Won't BFC Lite end up eating your lunch at some point in time?"

"Valid points that we went over thoroughly on the executive team and at the board level."

"I didn't mean to say—"

He shook his head with a smile to indicate that he was not offended.

"No, no, of course," he said. "Let me explain home-sourcing, as that may be somewhat easier. It's no secret that there are many lawyers who have families. And it is no secret that many of those lawyers wish to spend more time with their families. That is a very valid and commendable life decision for them to make.

"On the other hand, even with the innovative way we do business, there is a need for our people to be here on a full-time basis. On the third hand, if I had a third hand, and sometimes I wish I did, BFC hates to lose good lawyers. We refused to see this as an either/or situation. We didn't believe that there had to be a trade-off between working full-time or not working at all. There had to be another way to reconcile all concerns. Home-sourcing is the natural solution, at this point anyway. We had lawyers in whose abilities we already had total confidence, who had worked in our office and knew what we expected."

"Sure," Kim said. "So why lose them?"

Bowen nodded. "From logistics and security standpoints it worked well because our systems are cloud-based; nothing is kept on a separate computer and location is a nonfactor in terms of access. Equally true was the fact that most matters are done via phone with little face-to-face client contact, so again, location was a nonfactor. So, to your comment, why lose good people if we can make use of their talents and experience in a way that achieves their goals of family and professional challenge, while at the same time ensuring that we maintain a high degree of quality in an economical manner? We agree on what their fees will be and build that into our fee calculation. And do we expect that our home-sourcers will put the client first when they are on assignment? Yes, of course."

"I suppose," Kim added, "it also gives you elasticity in terms of capacity for overload situations without adding to your overhead costs."

"Correct. We're looking for a win/win/win; for ourselves, the client, and the lawyer."

"Sure, I can see that. But BFC Lite is a different kettle of fish—outside of the country, no prior experience within the firm structure, unknown lawyers working on the file, and data protection issues." Kim had a concerned tone. She hadn't used LPOs for any of her work for precisely these reasons.

"That's the standard response from our competitors and we're happy that they feel that way, because it just means we'll keep our advantage for an even longer period time."

Bowen took a sip from his wine glass and sat down on a long couch beside the glass guardrail, motioning Kim to position her wheelchair alongside to take advantage of the city view.

"I'll tell you what I told the board," Bowen said. "There are many routine matters in every legal practice that can be done by someone other than the main lawyer in charge. We look at this continually through our BFSigma program. At old-style firms, this work is given to clerks, students, junior lawyers, or other staff to reduce costs for the client. However, the persons involved are not inexpensive and they are billed out at a certain rate. They are still a cost center for the firm. To further reduce the costs and thereby increase profits, another way had to be found.

"LPOs provided that answer. They have skilled people that can do routine work at a rate that no one here could ever match. We could also see early on that LPOs were going to compete in the global legal marketplace and we needed to be partnered with an LPO that would give us that advantage, one that we could assimilate into our culture and increase their capabilities. The result was BFC Lite. Clients get the comfort of BFC's reputation combined with significant cost reductions."

Bowen smiled and continued.

"As much as we see competition here with other law firms, we see that LPOs, as they move up the food chain and take on more complex and sophisticated work, are also our competition. That day is coming sooner than anyone thinks and so we need to prepare for that day, because, as you mentioned, they have the potential to eat our lunch."

"But that doesn't change the fact they're an outside entity."

"Well they are and they aren't. We have a joint venture arrangement with shareholdings in it, board positions, local quality control, and privacy and confidentiality control. It has worked quite well for us and may very well move into a full acquisition—we will talk more about that at the board meeting tomorrow—to give us a captive entity with the cost savings and quality that we need. We have BFC people on the ground constantly in India; Chandri himself spends most of the year there. All new hires are seconded there to familiarize themselves with the operations and personnel, and to perform quality control functions."

"But you can only do that with senior people—senior new hires."

"Right, but we only hire senior laterals. In fact very early on we made a decision not to hire students and not to hire junior lawyers; our business model requires a certain level of professional maturity and experience. And, though we invest heavily in our professional development program, it's not designed for basic law training. Think of it at as a postgraduate level of training, going far beyond basic law. We don't need basic law programs, given the experience of our people."

"For now, I guess," Kim said. But if other firms start to move to our model of practice then I suppose we can shift on that item."

"BFC's ability to see the trends and react ahead of others will require us to do that to keep ourselves competitive," Bowen responded. "The interesting point is that with our use of BFC

Lite and home-sourcing we do not need large numbers of full-time lawyers. We do not hire reams of lawyers to see which ones sink or swim. That is a stupidly inefficient and ineffective way to do things and yet firms continue, like lemmings, to follow the same practice year after year. No other business runs that way. So, we don't have a student coordinator. We don't spend money on student brochures. We don't waste time interviewing on campus, or reviewing thousands of applications."

"It seems a bit harsh, given that's how you and I got our start in the profession."

"Sure, but how many students and first-year lawyers do you hire in-house for your company?"

"Point taken. None," Kim replied.

"We could spend time debating that law schools need to do a better job of preparing students for practice; create internships, apprenticeships, and so forth. But that is a topic for another day. And besides, since we suffer a very low attrition rate, our appetite for new lawyers is rather modest. If we can't accommodate increased work through our home-sourcers or BFC Lite, then, and only then, will we consider an appropriate lateral hire.

"The work we do in this office is high level bespoke[26] or project-management style of work that a junior lawyer is incapable of handling at the level that our clients demand. So you will not find anyone here who has less than five years of experience as a lawyer."

"Why do you think the attrition rate is so low?" she asked. "I mean, besides the fact that BFC is a fantastic place to work?"

"It's unusual for us to lose lawyers for two important reasons—both of which are based on our business model. First, once a lawyer works at BFC, she will find it hard to work in another firm that still clings to the old inefficiencies. She is used to being

---

[26] Richard Susskind uses this term as it relates to tailored legal services.

a manager and used to practicing law and looking at things in a new way. As Oliver Wendell Holmes said, 'A mind once stretched by a new idea never regains its original dimensions.' A lawyer who works with BFC cannot work anywhere else. Second, if that event actually happened, what do you think the chances are that any BFC clients would follow that lawyer to an old-style firm fraught with inefficiencies?"

"None."

"Exactly. And no firm is going to hire a senior lawyer without a book of business."

"But let's get back to BFC Lite." Kim didn't want to get sidetracked from an issue that she was very concerned about. "I assume that clients are aware of its use and have signed off."

"Absolutely. They are also aware that we operate in the cloud and use SaaS.[27] It's part of our pitch to clients that we operate in the manner of a good business and make use of all opportunities to provide better service at competitive pricing; we revel in our efficiencies. Our materials and website are all very clear about how work is done and by whom. Clients come to us because of the way we run our business. So, in answer to your question, do they know and do they sign off? The answer is yes."

"I see," she said.

"In fact, we have clients asking to use BFC Lite! As you can imagine, there is a fair amount of routine work that we do for many clients. Financial institutions are probably the most obvious example. And we would like to keep that kind of work, but the reality is that the only way to keep it is through BFC Lite. It's bad enough that we lose work due to conflicts, but to lose work because we can't do it in a cost-effective manner is unthinkable

---

[27] See Appendix B for guidelines by the North Carolina Bar Association in connection with the use of SaaS by law firms, and those by the New York Bar Association on lawyers using the cloud.

here. BFC Lite gives us the ability to increase the range of services we offer our client without sacrificing quality and profits."

"The thin edge of the wedge," she said, nodding. "Once you lose work to an unaffiliated LPO, you know that they'll be working hard to get more work and increase their level of sophistication. You're right, ignoring the trend would be dangerous."

"Our connection with BFC Lite," Bowen added, "also provides some comfort to the client in terms of accountability. Clients are confident in BFC's quality and our ability to ensure that our team in India is top notch. And to tell you the truth, we want to grow the BFC Lite side of things, as it makes sense for our India team to do as much work as possible given their price points. The more that we can have them do over there, the less need we have to hire expensive personnel here, which would then require us to find larger premises, and so on. If we can manage our growth in ways that do not require huge overhead costs, why wouldn't we do it?"

"And I suppose from BFC Lite's point of view," Kim added, "the lawyers there see it as excellent professional development to increase their skills, which in turn, gives clients greater confidence."

"Correct," Bowen said. "It all feeds on itself. Now, since we're on the topic, what is your initial take on our BFC Lite white-labeling proposal in the board package?"

"I'm on the fence with that," she said. The proposal, as she recalled it, was very aggressive, perhaps even insane; typical BFC. Bowen had proposed white-labeling BFC Lite's work to other law firms. The work would be done by BFC Lite, but labeled as if it had come from the local firms, allowing those firms to retain routine work from their clients and not lose it to LPOs. There would be transparency to the client in terms of the fact that work was being done offshore, but the client would have the added comfort that law firms were involved. The proposal required the client confidentiality to be sorted out through appropriate mechanisms, but Bowen viewed these as merely details to be ironed out, not barriers.

"Ah," he said. "Which means you don't like it. Fair enough. Then, back to your point about students, to some extent BFC Lite is a farm team as it were, of juniors and students—just not in this country."

"You're quite the patriot!" she said with sarcasm.

"I don't think that anyone will be crying for lawyers in this country," he said, looking about. "In any event, students here are free to apply to our India operations. That will cause quite a stir, but change often does. It's the price to be paid for years of complacency and a failure to recognize the shift in the landscape; firms can no longer ignore the inefficiencies."

"I see your point," Kim replied.

"Well, as much as I enjoy leading BFC in innovation, my overall plan is to force change in the legal profession at large," Bowen said. "The more successful that BFC becomes, the more other firms will have to sit up and take notice.

"All our board members see what we do with complete transparency; you see the numbers, the costs, and the profits. More importantly, you see how things can be if a firm takes a different approach. That knowledge does not remain in the boardroom when you exit. It stays with you and will affect your relationship with your own outside counsel. It will cause you to start to question how they operate and presumably you will start pushing them to change their ways in order to retain your business.

"Multiply that by the eight other board members, and the ones that replace them. Law firms themselves are far too cautious and incremental to make these types of changes on their own. They need to be prodded by clients and they need to lose business to other legal service providers. Only then will meaningful change occur."

"For some, that change will come too late."

"No question about that. Some firms will disappear. Again, few tears will be shed."

A waiter came up to the two of them.

"Excuse me," he said bowing to them both. "It's time, sir."

"I guess the directors want the evening to formally begin," Bowen said to Kim. "Shall we?" he said motioning her to a long table set for dinner. At his direction, she wheeled herself in to the space to his right.

As they dined, Bowen made a point of including Kim in every conversation he held with other nearby board members, always asking her opinion on new ideas and concerns. The director sitting opposite her mentioned that being on the board of BFC made him extremely happy because he was finally building something that he would love to use.

Before dessert was served Bowen stood up and called for the attention of the group. Speech time, Kim thought.

Bowen started with the usual sentiments of welcoming everyone and thanking them for taking time to come to dinner. His words then took on a more serious tone.

"For us at BFC," Bowen said, "independent directors are the key to keeping us honest in terms of our strategic vision of the firm. You are among our most important strategic assets. You are the ones to safeguard the long-term viability of the firm regardless of the individual aspirations of the lawyers within it.

"You are the ones that ensure that we are sustainable long after the lawyers working now are gone. You are the ones that ensure that proper care is taken in terms of retained earnings to maintain our innovations, so that we constantly invest in improvement and can weather all storms that come up us.

"I want BFC to be around forever. Not because of my own personal egotistical needs, but because BFC is, and should continue to be, greater than the sum of its parts.

"Now, I do have an announcement. I have spoken to the chair prior to this so as to not take her by surprise."

Bowen paused for effect.

"I am stepping down in favor of a non-lawyer CEO."

The directors gasped. Bowen waved his hands to calm them and to allow him to finish.

"BFC is mature enough as an organization, both in thought and in management style, that the silly notion that a lawyer is required to run the organization is no longer valid. We've broken from the old-school firm model and transitioned into a finely tuned company.

"There's a reason why many entrepreneurs are replaced as CEO of their company after a number of years. They had the technical skills to get the ball rolling and to build up the company based on their skills, but then they plateau. They don't have the skills to run a mature enterprise and so proper management needs to be brought in to bring the company to the next level. In the same way that you do not want engineers running a public transit system, nor pilots running airlines, lawyers should not be running law firms. A business-minded CEO is the next logical step in our evolution.

"Now, I'm not leaving tomorrow. I will actively take part in the search for a replacement, along with the appropriate search committee from the board, to find a professional manager with some legal background. That selection is critical to the future of BFC and as a shareholder I do have an interest in the long-term viability of BFC.

"I don't anticipate any issues from our lawyers and staff. I have had a non-legal role in BFC for ten years now and so they are used to having a non-practicing CEO within a corporate structure. This will also be a prerequisite to eventually taking BFC public. Currently our jurisdiction does not allow a law firm to be owned by outside shareholders, but I believe that will change and we will be ready for that change with the type of proven structure that will instill confidence in shareholders.

"And in answer to the obvious question of what lies next for me, we can have detailed discussions after dinner," he said, motioning up at the starry sky. "It is a beautiful night, after all." He then smiled the sort of mischievous smile that small children make when they can't hold back a secret. "Well maybe I will give you a few highlights."

The group laughed.

"There are two ideas that I am looking at pursuing and I would welcome your feedback. First, the creation of a Facebook-type of product for law firms that would allow communication among all lawyers in our jurisdiction, the housing of all transactional documents—including the ability to draft and comment—as well as the transfer of funds, all housed in one secure cloud environment. This way we all play in the same space. Which should make interaction among us easier."

There were some murmurs from the crowd as to whether that would be viable.

"I am also looking at the concept of franchised law offices for the legal needs of the average person. There needs to be greater access to justice for the average person on the street—and the best way to achieve that is through the efficiencies that we have learned about and utilize at BFC."

Bowen concluded with some funny anecdotes about the creation of the firm and about some of the directors, before thanking them all for their work. A few of the more senior directors walked over to him for handshakes, compliments, and chiding for not letting them know his plans in advance.

Kim stared out at the office towers in the distance trying to take in what had just happened. An innovative firm was losing its visionary CEO. This could, she thought, be a very interesting time to be part of BFC as it searched for its first non-lawyer CEO. Bowen was definitely correct: all CEOs, no matter how visionary, have a shelf life. Perhaps it was time for professional managers to be added to the mix so that BFC lawyers can do what they best—practice law—and leave the business end of things to those with proper training.

She called the waiter over and ordered another drink.

Kowtor Industries Outside Counsel Expense and Disbursement Policy

Kowtor will pay only actual expenses made by the law firm.

The law firm must pass along to Kowtor all discounts and rebates that it receives, or that are readily available to the law firm from its suppliers on all expenses, including travel.

Kowtor will, from time to time, audit expenses, so the law firm must keep a record of all expenses charged to Kowtor.

Kowtor considers the following items to be part of law firm overhead, and therefore Kowtor will not pay:

1. Secretarial or staff time, or overtime (unless Kowtor has approved this expense in advance);
2. Library staff time (unless such time is more economical to Kowtor as a substitute for time that would otherwise be billed by an attorney or legal assistant);
3. Transportation between home and office;
4. Meals for lawyers and staff (except during travel);
5. Telephone charges, including cell phone charges, and any charges for calls to, or from, airplanes;
6. Fax charges;
7. Charges for communication or deliveries between the law firm's offices;

8. Office supplies (including tabs, binders, dividers, CDs/DVDs, etc.);

9. Postage;

10. Charges for scanning documents, CD/DVD duplication or "mastering," word processing, or any internal charge for document production or printing, unless previously agreed by Kowtor;

11. Time spent on conflict checks, preparing bills, or responding to questions about bills;

12. Any charges for "document retrieval" or "filing";

13. All other "office" or "overhead" charges;

14. Any travel time; and

15. First class transportation.

Kowtor reimburses for business class transportation only for those flights over five hours in duration in one aircraft.

The law firm is to use Kowtor's travel department to make travel arrangements and must use vendors where Kowtor has negotiated favorable rates. If the law firm is unable to use Kowtor's travel department, then it must take advantage of discounts and special rates when possible. It is not acceptable to seek reimbursement for a higher fare on a similar route or to pay a higher hotel rate to maximize frequent traveler points or other promotions that benefit the traveler or the law firm and not Kowtor. Kowtor pays for reasonable business hotels, but will not pay for luxury hotels (unless the law firm obtains prior approval from Kowtor). Also, Kowtor does not pay for luxury meals or alcohol.

For large copying jobs approved by Kowtor, the law firm must use an outside service or give Kowtor the opportunity to arrange for copies ourselves where meaningful savings are available.

Some Ethical Considerations for Law Firms Using SaaS and the Cloud

Software as a service and cloud computing are areas that are rife with arguments over the duty and obligations of lawyers in connection with client information. BFC takes great care in maintaining its ethical obligations while using new, efficient and innovative forms of technology including SaaS and the cloud. The materials in this Appendix are fine examples of how some bar associations and law societies[28] recognize the need for lawyers

---

[28] See also the following: Iowa State Bar Association Committee on Ethics and Practice Guidelines: Ethics Opinion 11-01 Use of Software as a Service – Cloud Computing (9/9/11) http://iowabar.org/associations/4664/files/Ethics%20Opinion%202011-01%20--%20Software%20as%20a%20Service%20-%20Cloud%20Computing.pdf. Pennsylvania Bar Association Committee on Legal Ethics and Professional Responsibility: Informal Opinion 2010-60 (1/11/11; available online to Pennsylvania Bar members only) State Bar of Arizona Ethics Opinion 09-04: Confidentiality; Maintaining Client Files; Electronic Storage; Internet http://www.myazbar.org/ethics/opinionview.cfm?id=704 Maine State Bar Professional Ethics Commission: "Client Confidences: Confidential firm data held electronically and handled by technicians for third-party vendors;" Opinion 194 (6/30/08) http://www.maine.gov/tools/whatsnew/index.php?topic=mebar_overseers_ethics_opinions&id=86894&v=article. New Jersey Bar Advisory Committee on Professional Ethics: "Electronic Storage and Access of Client Files;" Opinion 701 (4/24/06) http://lawlibrary.rutgers.edu/ethics/acpe/acp701_1.html. State Bar of Arizona Ethics Opinion 05-04: Electronic Storage; Confidentiality (07/05) http://www.myazbar.org/Ethics/opinionview.cfm?id=523

to be able to take advantage of new technology in a manner that keeps them ethically grounded without being burdened by new rules. The Law Society of British Columbia also came out with a report on cloud computing in July, 2011[29] which comes to a similar conclusion. In a nutshell, it is up to each firm to conduct proper due diligence on new technology and service providers to appropriately manage risks to client confidentiality, keeping in mind that there is no duty to keep data infallibly secure.

2011 Formal Ethics Opinion 6 – North Carolina State Bar Subscribing to Software as a Service While Fulfilling the Duties of Confidentiality and Preservation of Client Property
January 27, 2012

Opinion rules that a lawyer may contract with a vendor of software as a service provided the lawyer uses reasonable care to safeguard confidential client information.

Inquiry #1:

Much of software development, including the specialized software used by lawyers for case or practice management, document management, and billing/financial management, is moving to the "software as a service" (SaaS) model. The American Bar Association's Legal Technology Resource Center explains SaaS as follows:

---

[29] Law Society of British Columbia, *Report of the Cloud Computing Working Group*, July 15, 2011, http://www.lawsociety.bc.ca/docs/publications/reports/CloudComputing.pdf For further information readers can also see the International Legal Technical Standards Organization at www.iltso.org and its recent report on this area http://iltso.org/iltso/Standards_files/ILTSO%20Master%20Document%202011%20Final.pdf

> *SaaS is distinguished from traditional software in several ways. Rather than installing the software to your computer or the firm's server, SaaS is accessed via a web browser (like Internet Explorer or FireFox) over the internet. Data is stored in the vendor's data center rather than on the firm's computers. Upgrades and updates, both major and minor, are rolled out continuously...SaaS is usually sold on a subscription model, meaning that users pay a monthly fee rather than purchasing a license up front.*[30]

Instances of SaaS software extend beyond the practice management sphere addressed above, and can include technologies as far-ranging as web-based email programs, online legal research software, online backup and storage, text messaging/SMS (short message service), voicemail on mobile or VoIP phones, online communication over social media, and beyond.

SaaS for law firms may involve the storage of a law firm's data, including client files, billing information, and work product, on remote servers rather than on the law firm's own computer and, therefore, outside the direct control of the firm's lawyers. Lawyers have duties to safeguard confidential client information, including protecting that information from unauthorized disclosure, and to protect client property from destruction, degradation, or loss (whether from system failure, natural disaster, or dissolution of a vendor's business). Lawyers also have a continuing need to retrieve client data in a form that is usable outside of a vendor's product.[31] Given these duties and needs, may a law firm use SaaS?

---

[30] FYI: Software as a Service (SaaS) for Lawyers, ABA Legal Technology Resource Center at abanet.org/tech/ ltrc/fyidocs/saas.html.

[31] *Id.*

Opinion #1:

Yes, provided steps are taken to minimize the risk of inadvertent or unauthorized disclosure of confidential client information and to protect client property, including the information in a client's file, from risk of loss.

The use of the internet to transmit and store client information presents significant challenges. In this complex and technical environment, a lawyer must be able to fulfill the fiduciary obligations to protect confidential client information and property from risk of disclosure and loss. The lawyer must protect against security weaknesses unique to the internet, particularly "end-user" vulnerabilities found in the lawyer's own law office. The lawyer must also engage in periodic education about ever-changing security risks presented by the internet.

Rule 1.6 of the Rules of Professional Conduct states that a lawyer may not reveal information acquired during the professional relationship with a client unless the client gives informed consent or the disclosure is impliedly authorized to carry out the representation. Comment [17] explains, "A lawyer must act competently to safeguard information relating to the representation of a client against inadvertent or unauthorized disclosure by the lawyer or other persons who are participating in the representation of the client or who are subject to the lawyer's supervision." Comment [18] adds that, when transmitting confidential client information, a lawyer must take "reasonable precautions to prevent the information from coming into the hands of unintended recipients."

Rule 1.15 requires a lawyer to preserve client property, including information in a client's file such as client documents and lawyer work product, from risk of loss due to destruction, degradation, or loss. *See also* RPC 209 (noting the "general fiduciary duty to safeguard the property of a client"), RPC 234 (requiring the storage of a client's original documents with legal significance in a safe place or their return to the client), and 98 FEO 15 (requiring exercise of lawyer's "due care" when selecting depository bank for trust account).

Although a lawyer has a professional obligation to protect confidential information from unauthorized disclosure, the Ethics Committee has long held that this duty does not compel any particular mode of handling confidential information nor does it prohibit the employment of vendors whose services may involve the handling of documents or data containing client information. *See* RPC 133 (stating there is no requirement that firm's waste paper be shredded if lawyer ascertains that persons or entities responsible for the disposal employ procedures that effectively minimize the risk of inadvertent or unauthorized disclosure of confidential information). Moreover, while the duty of confidentiality applies to lawyers who choose to use technology to communicate, "this obligation does not require that a lawyer use only infallibly secure methods of communication." RPC 215. Rather, the lawyer must use reasonable care to select a mode of communication that, in light of the circumstances, will best protect confidential client information and the lawyer must advise effected parties if there is reason to believe that the chosen communications technology presents an unreasonable risk to confidentiality.

Furthermore, in 2008 FEO 5, the committee held that the use of a web-based document management system that allows both the law firm and the client access to the client's file is permissible:

> provided the lawyer can fulfill his obligation to protect the confidential information of all clients. A lawyer must take steps to minimize the risk that confidential client information will be disclosed to

other clients or to third parties. *See* RPC 133 and RPC 215…. A security code access procedure that only allows a client to access its own confidential information would be an appropriate measure to protect confidential client information…. If the law firm will be contracting with a third party to maintain the web-based management system, the law firm must ensure that the third party also employs measures which effectively minimize the risk that confidential information might be lost or disclosed. *See* RPC 133.

In a recent ethics opinion, the Arizona State Bar's Committee on the Rules of Professional Conduct concurred with the interpretation set forth in North Carolina's 2008 FEO 5 by holding that an Arizona law firm may use an online file storage and retrieval system that allows clients to access their files over the internet provided the firm takes reasonable precautions to protect the security and confidentiality of client documents and information.[32]

In light of the above, the Ethics Committee concludes that a law firm may use SaaS if reasonable care is taken to minimize the risks of inadvertent disclosure of confidential information and to protect the security of client information and client files. A lawyer must fulfill the duties to protect confidential client information and to safeguard client files by applying the same diligence and competency to manage the risks of SaaS that the lawyer is required to apply when representing clients.

No opinion is expressed on the business question of whether SaaS is suitable for a particular law firm.

---

[32] Paraphrasing the description of a lawyer's duties in Arizona State Bar Committee on Rules of Professional Conduct, Opinion 09-04 (Dec. 9, 2009).

Inquiry #2:

Are there measures that a lawyer or law firm should consider when assessing a SaaS vendor or seeking to minimize the security risks of SaaS?

Opinion #2:

This opinion does not set forth specific security requirements because mandatory security measures would create a false sense of security in an environment where the risks are continually changing. Instead, due diligence and frequent and regular education are required.

Although a lawyer may use nonlawyers outside of the firm to assist in rendering legal services to clients, Rule 5.3(a) requires the lawyer to make reasonable efforts to ensure that the services are provided in a manner that is compatible with the professional obligations of the lawyer. The extent of this obligation when using a SaaS vendor to store and manipulate confidential client information will depend upon the experience, stability, and reputation of the vendor. Given the rapidity with which computer technology changes, law firms are encouraged to consult periodically with professionals competent in the area of online security. Some recommended security measures are listed below.

- Inclusion in the SaaS vendor's Terms of Service or Service Level Agreement, or in a separate agreement between the SaaS vendor and the lawyer or law firm, of an agreement on how the vendor will handle confidential client information in keeping with the lawyer's professional responsibilities.
- If the lawyer terminates use of the SaaS product, the SaaS vendor goes out of business, or the service otherwise has a break in continuity, the law firm will have a method for

retrieving the data, the data will be available in a non-proprietary format that the law firm can access, or the firm will have access to the vendor's software or source code. The SaaS vendor is contractually required to return or destroy the hosted data promptly at the request of the law firm.

- Careful review of the terms of the law firm's user or license agreement with the SaaS vendor including the security policy.
- Evaluation of the SaaS vendor's (or any third party data hosting company's) measures for safeguarding the security and confidentiality of stored data including, but not limited to, firewalls, encryption techniques, socket security features, and intrusion-detection systems.[33]
- Evaluation of the extent to which the SaaS vendor backs up hosted data.

New York State Bar Association
Committee on Professional Ethics
Opinion 842 (9/10/10)

Topic: Using an outside online storage provider to store client confidential information.

---

[33] A firewall is a system (which may consist of hardware, software, or both) that protects the resources of a private network from users of other networks. Encryption techniques are methods for ciphering messages into a foreign format that can only be deciphered using keys and reverse encryption algorithms. A socket security feature is a commonly-used protocol for managing the security of message transmission on the internet. An intrusion detection system is a system (which may consist of hardware, software, or both) that monitors network and/or system activities for malicious activities and produces reports for management.

Digest: A lawyer may use an online data storage system to store and back up client confidential information provided that the lawyer takes reasonable care to ensure that confidentiality will be maintained in a manner consistent with the lawyer's obligations under Rule 1.6. In addition, the lawyer should stay abreast of technological advances to ensure that the storage system remains sufficiently advanced to protect the client's information, and should monitor the changing law of privilege to ensure that storing the information online will not cause loss or waiver of any privilege.

Rules: 1.4, 1.6(a), 1.6(c)
Question

1. May a lawyer use an online system to store a client's confidential information without violating the duty of confidentiality or any other duty? If so, what steps should the lawyer take to ensure that the information is sufficiently secure?

Opinion

2. Various companies offer online computer data storage systems that are maintained on an array of Internet servers located around the world. (The array of Internet servers that store the data is often called the "cloud.") A solo practitioner would like to use one of these online "cloud" computer data storage systems to store client confidential information. The lawyer's aim is to ensure that his clients' information will not be lost if something happens to the lawyer's own computers. The online data storage system is password-protected and the data stored in the online system is encrypted.

3. A discussion of confidential information implicates Rule 1.6 of the New York Rules of Professional Conduct (the "Rules"), the general rule governing confidentiality. Rule 1.6(a) provides as follows:

A lawyer shall not knowingly reveal confidential information . . . or use such information to the disadvantage of a client or for the advantage of a lawyer or a third person, unless:

(1) the client gives informed consent, as defined in Rule 1.0(j);

(2) the disclosure is impliedly authorized to advance the best interests of the client and is either reasonable under the circumstances or customary in the professional community; or

(3) the disclosure is permitted by paragraph (b).

4. The obligation to preserve client confidential information extends beyond merely prohibiting an attorney from revealing confidential information without client consent. A lawyer must also take reasonable care to affirmatively protect a client's confidential information. See N.Y. County 733 (2004) (an attorney "must diligently preserve the client's confidences, whether reduced to digital format, paper, or otherwise"). As a New Jersey ethics committee observed, even when a lawyer wants a closed client file to be destroyed, "[s]imply placing the files in the trash would not suffice. Appropriate steps must be taken to ensure that confidential and privileged information remains protected and not available to third parties." New Jersey Opinion (2006), *quoting* New Jersey Opinion 692 (2002).

5. In addition, Rule 1.6(c) provides that an attorney must "exercise reasonable care to prevent . . . others whose services are utilized by the lawyer from disclosing or using

confidential information of a client" except to the extent disclosure is permitted by Rule 1.6(b). Accordingly, a lawyer must take reasonable affirmative steps to guard against the risk of inadvertent disclosure by others who are working under the attorney's supervision or who have been retained by the attorney to assist in providing services to the client. We note, however, that exercising "reasonable care" under Rule 1.6 does not mean that the lawyer guarantees that the information is secure from *any* unauthorized access.

6. To date, no New York ethics opinion has addressed the ethics of *storing* confidential information online. However, in N.Y. State 709 (1998) this Committee addressed the duty to preserve a client's confidential information when *transmitting* such information electronically. Opinion 709 concluded that lawyers may transmit confidential information by e-mail, but cautioned that "lawyers must always act reasonably in choosing to use e-mail for confidential communications." The Committee also warned that the exercise of reasonable care may differ from one case to the next. Accordingly, when a lawyer is on notice that the confidential information being transmitted is "of such an extraordinarily sensitive nature that it is reasonable to use only a means of communication that is completely under the lawyer's control, the lawyer must select a more secure means of communication than unencrypted Internet e-mail." *See also* Rule 1.6, cmt. 17 (a lawyer "must take reasonable precautions" to prevent information coming into the hands of unintended recipients when transmitting information relating to the representation, but is not required to use special security measures if the means of communicating provides a reasonable expectation of privacy).

7. Ethics advisory opinions in several other states have approved the use of electronic storage of client files provided that sufficient precautions are in place. *See, e.g.,* New Jersey Opinion 701 (2006) (lawyer may use electronic filing system whereby all documents are scanned into a digitized format and entrusted to someone outside the firm provided that the lawyer exercises "reasonable care," which includes entrusting documents to a third party with an enforceable obligation to preserve confidentiality and security, and employing available technology to guard against reasonably foreseeable attempts to infiltrate data); Arizona Opinion 05-04 (2005) (electronic storage of client files is permissible provided lawyers and law firms "take competent and reasonable steps to assure that the client's confidences are not disclosed to third parties through theft or inadvertence"); *see also* Arizona Opinion 09-04 (2009) (lawyer may provide clients with an online file storage and retrieval system that clients may access, provided lawyer takes reasonable precautions to protect security and confidentiality and lawyer periodically reviews security measures as technology advances over time to ensure that the confidentiality of client information remains reasonably protected).

8. Because the inquiring lawyer will use the online data storage system for the purpose of preserving client information—a purpose both related to the retention and necessary to providing legal services to the client—using the online system is consistent with conduct that this Committee has deemed ethically permissible. *See* N.Y. State 473 (1977) (absent client's objection, lawyer may provide confidential information to outside service agency for legitimate purposes relating to the representation provided that the

lawyer exercises care in the selection of the agency and cautions the agency to keep the information confidential); cf. NY CPLR 4548 (privileged communication does not lose its privileged character solely because it is communicated by electronic means or because "persons necessary for the delivery or facilitation of such electronic communication may have access to" its contents).

9. We conclude that a lawyer may use an online "cloud" computer data backup system to store client files provided that the lawyer takes reasonable care to ensure that the system is secure and that client confidentiality will be maintained. "Reasonable care" to protect a client's confidential information against unauthorized disclosure may include consideration of the following steps:

- Ensuring that the online data storage provider has an enforceable obligation to preserve confidentiality and security, and that the provider will notify the lawyer if served with process requiring the production of client information;

- Investigating the online data storage provider's security measures, policies, recoverability methods, and other procedures to determine if they are adequate under the circumstances;

- Employing available technology to guard against reasonably foreseeable attempts to infiltrate the data that is stored; and/or

- investigating the storage provider's ability to purge and wipe any copies of the data, and to move the data to a different host, if the lawyer becomes dissatisfied with the storage provider or for other reasons changes storage providers.

10. Technology and the security of stored data are changing rapidly. Even after taking some or all of these steps (or similar steps), therefore, the lawyer should periodically reconfirm that the provider's security measures remain effective in light of advances in technology. If the lawyer learns information suggesting that the security measures used by the online data storage provider are insufficient to adequately protect the confidentiality of client information, or if the lawyer learns of any breach of confidentiality by the online storage provider, then the lawyer must investigate whether there has been any breach of his or her own clients' confidential information, notify any affected clients, and discontinue use of the service unless the lawyer receives assurances that any security issues have been sufficiently remediated. See Rule 1.4 (mandating communication with clients); *see also* N.Y. State 820 (2008) (addressing Web-based email services).

11. Not only technology itself but also the law relating to technology and the protection of confidential communications is changing rapidly. Lawyers using online storage systems (and electronic means of communication generally) should monitor these legal developments, especially regarding instances when using technology may waive an otherwise applicable privilege. *See, e.g., City of Ontario, Calif. v. Quon*, 130 S. Ct. 2619, 177 L.Ed.2d 216 (2010) (holding that City did not violate Fourth Amendment when it reviewed transcripts of messages sent and received by police officers on police department pagers); *Scott v. Beth Israel Medical Center*, 17 Misc. 3d 934, 847 N.Y.S.2d 436 (N.Y. Sup. 2007) (e-mails between hospital employee and his personal attorneys were not privileged because employer's policy regarding computer

use and e-mail monitoring stated that employees had no reasonable expectation of privacy in e-mails sent over the employer's e-mail server). *But see Stengart v. Loving Care Agency, Inc.*, 201 N.J. 300, 990 A.2d 650 (2010) (despite employer's e-mail policy stating that company had right to review and disclose all information on "the company's media systems and services" and that e-mails were "not to be considered private or personal" to any employees, company violated employee's attorney-client privilege by reviewing e-mails sent to employee's personal attorney on employer's laptop through employee's personal, password-protected e-mail account).

12. This Committee's prior opinions have addressed the disclosure of confidential information in metadata and the perils of practicing law over the Internet. We have noted in those opinions that the duty to "exercise reasonable care" to prevent disclosure of confidential information "may, in some circumstances, call for the lawyer to stay abreast of technological advances and the potential risks" in transmitting information electronically. N.Y. State 782 (2004), *citing* N.Y. State 709 (1998) (when conducting trademark practice over the Internet, lawyer had duty to "stay abreast of this evolving technology to assess any changes in the likelihood of interception as well as the availability of improved technologies that may reduce such risks at reasonable cost"); *see also* N.Y. State 820 (2008) (same in context of using e-mail service provider that scans e-mails to generate computer advertising). The same duty to stay current with the technological advances applies to a lawyer's contemplated use of an online data storage system.

Conclusion

13. A lawyer may use an online data storage system to store and
    back up client confidential information provided that the
    lawyer takes reasonable care to ensure that confidentiality
    is maintained in a manner consistent with the lawyer's
    obligations under Rule 1.6. A lawyer using an online
    storage provider should take reasonable care to protect
    confidential information, and should exercise reasonable
    care to prevent others whose services are utilized by the
    lawyer from disclosing or using confidential information
    of a client. In addition, the lawyer should stay abreast of
    technological advances to ensure that the storage system
    remains sufficiently advanced to protect the client's
    information, and the lawyer should monitor the changing
    law of privilege to ensure that storing information in
    the "cloud" will not waive or jeopardize any privilege
    protecting the information.

Suggested Reading Material

Many writers helped shape the thoughts in this book. The following are those materials that provided me with the greatest assistance in preparing this book and I commend them to any lawyer who is serious about creating her own profitable law firm.

BOOKS AND JOURNAL ARTICLES

Yilmaz Argüden, Boardroom Secrets (Palgrave Macmillan 2009)

Barbara J. Boake & Rick A. Kathuria, Project Management for Lawyers (Ark Group 2011).

Roger Martin, The Opposable Mind (Harv. Bus. Press 2009).

Roger Martin, The Design of Business (Harv. Bus. Press 2009).

Stephen Mayson, Making Sense of Law Firms (Blackstone Press Ltd. 1997).

Stephen Mayson, Law Firm Strategy (Oxford Univ. Press 2007).

Matthew Parsons, Effective Knowledge Management for Law Firms (Oxford Univ. Press 2004).

Michael Posner, *What is Strategy?*, HARV. BUS. REV., Nov./Dec. 1996.

BOB PROPST, THE OFFICE: A FACILITY BASED ON CHANGE.

Isadore Sharp, *Notes for an Address by Isadore Sharp to the Ivey School of Business*, 2006 Leader Award, Sept. 21, 2006, Toronto, Canada.

SIMON SINEK, START WITH WHY (Penguin 2009).

RICHARD SUSSKIND, THE FUTURE OF LAW (Oxford Univ. Press 1996).

RICHARD SUSSKIND, THE END OF LAWYERS? (Oxford Univ. Press 2008).

NON-BOOK RESOURCES

There are a growing number of commentators on innovation in the legal profession. The following is a sampling of resources available on the internet that discuss aspects of the legal profession's future.

Above and Beyond KM—http://aboveandbeyondkm.com/

Adam Smith—http://www.adamsmithesq.com/

Amazing Firms Amazing Practices—http://www.gerryriskin.com/

Association of Corporate Counsel—http://www.acc.com/

At the Intersection—http://www.pamwoldow.com/

Attorney at Work—http://www.attorneyatwork.com/

Computational Legal Studies—http://computationallegalstudies.com/

Connie Crosby—http://conniecrosby.blogspot.ca/

ILTA KM—http://km.iltanet.org/

In Search of Perfect Client Service—http://www.patrickjlamb.com/

John Flood's Random Academic Thoughts—http://www.johnflood.com/blog/

Law 21—http://www.law21.ca/

Lawyer Watch—http://lawyerwatch.wordpress.com/

Legal Futures—http://www.legalfutures.co.uk/blog

Legal Mosaic - http://legalmosaic.com/blog/

Legal Onramp—http://legalonramp.com/

Prism Legal—http://www.prismlegal.com/wordpress/

Richard Susskind—http://www.susskind.com/

Robert Ambrogi's LawSites—http://www.lawsitesblog.com/

Stephen Mayson—http://stephenmayson.com/

The Intelligent Challenge—http://intelligentchallenge.com/

3 Geeks and a Law Blog—http://www.geeklawblog.com/

Thoughtful Legal Management—http://thoughtfullaw.com/

Virtual Law Practice—http://virtuallawpractice.org/

Printed in the United States
By Bookmasters